LONGMAN LITERATURE

Shirley Valentine

Willy Russell

Editor: Roy Blatchford

Longman Literature Shakespeare
Series editor: Roy Blatchford
Consultant: Jackie Head

Macbeth   0 582 08827 5 (paper)
              0 582 24592 3 (cased)
Romeo and Juliet   0 582 08836 4 (paper)
                      0 582 24591 5 (cased)
The Merchant of Venice   0 582 08835 6 (paper)
                           0 582 24593 1 (cased)
A Midsummer Night's Dream   0 582 08833 X (paper)
                              0 582 24590 7 (cased)
Julius Caesar   0 582 08828 3 (paper)
                  0 582 24589 3 (cased)
Twelfth Night   0 582 08834 8 (paper)
Othello   0 582 09719 3 (paper)
King Lear   0 582 09718 5 (paper)
Hamlet   0 582 09720 7 (paper)
Henry V   0 582 22584 1 (paper)
The Tempest   0 582 22583 3 (paper)
Henry IV Part 1   0 582 23660 6 (paper)
As You Like It   0 582 23661 4 (paper)
Richard III   0 582 23663 0 (paper)

Longman Literature
Series editor: Roy Blatchford

Plays

Alan Ayckbourn   *Absurd Person Singular*   0 582 06020 6
Arthur Miller   *An Enemy of the People*   0 582 09717 7
J B Priestley   *An Inspector Calls*   0 582 06012 5
Terence Rattigan   *The Winslow Boy*   0 582 06019 2
Willy Russell   *Educating Rita*   0 582 06013 3
                 Shirley Valentine   0 582 08173 4
Peter Shaffer   *The Royal Hunt of the Sun*   0 582 06014 1
                 Equus   0 582 09712 6
Bernard Shaw   *Arms and the Man*   0 582 07785 0
                Pygmalion   0 582 06015 X
                Saint Joan   0 582 07786 9
Oscar Wilde   *The Importance of Being Earnest*   0 582 07784 2

Other titles in the Longman Literatures series are listed on page 127.

Contents

The writer on writing

An interview with Willy Russell

This interview on screen and stage writing, with particular reference to the screenplay of *Shirley Valentine,* was recorded on 12 November 1990 in Liverpool.

Interviewer: What caused you to turn your stage play *Shirley Valentine* into a film?

Willy Russell: I had some time available because this play had opened in Liverpool, and because of different logistical and practical difficulties, like availability of a suitable theatre, director and actress for a London production, I was waiting around, and at a time like that I can't begin work on a new play but I was itching to do *some* work. In that period I'd remembered that Lewis Gilbert, who'd made the film *Educating Rita,* had been on at me, since he'd seen it [*Shirley Valentine*] in Liverpool, really about eighteen months previously, he'd been badgering me to let him make it as a film. I'd had one or two problems with the film of *Educating Rita* so I went to see Lewis. I said, 'Look these were my problems on *Educating Rita,* if the same problems are not going to occur on *Shirley Valentine* then we can film it and I'll sit down and write the screenplay.' Lewis assured me that we wouldn't have the same problem, so I sat down and I wrote the screenplay.

Interviewer: Did you work closely with the director on the adaptation from stage to screen?

Willy Russell: When we worked on *Educating Rita* I'd written quite a lot of film before but I'd not written a feature film that had actually been made – I'd written films like *Our Day Out* for the BBC and a long serialised film for Yorkshire TV, *One Summer,* and yet this was my first feature film, *Educating Rita.*

Lewis Gilbert the producer/director who was then working from Paris asked me to go over and spend a week with him and I didn't quite know what this was going to be for. So I went to Paris and I found that I would meet with Lewis in the morning and he would talk about the play and how he wanted to see the film. I realised within three seconds of this process that that was not the way I worked. But here was a veteran film director, who did work in this way and obviously expected me to. Here was a man who'd been making films for longer than I'd been alive and so I hardly felt in a position to question his methods. Equally, though, I knew that this way of working was not right for me.

When I come to write a film, even from an original play, I have to become fired with the same sort of imaginative, creative flow as I'd had when writing the original. It seemed to me this rather dry mapping out of the scenes that would be in the film was, for me, a counter productive way of working, good for some screenwriters I know, but not me. I wasn't insulting Lewis or being rude to Lewis; it was just a fact that we were very new to each other and I thought that the best way to convince him of the way I worked was to do the work itself. I took these notes but didn't use them when I got back to England and began work.

I was about thirty pages into the screenplay when Lewis phoned to ask, 'How are things going?' I said, 'Fine Lewis but you do know that I'm not following anything in this schemata we thrashed out in Paris.' There was horror on the other end of the phone – I mean I felt my telephone turn molten red and so said, 'Look, I've got a longhand version here (I write in longhand first of all, I don't type out). There's no point me sending it to you, it's illegible, so I'll come down to London and read to you the thirty pages.' I set off and with every mile nearer I got to London I questioned endlessly whether he would respond to this, but I knew that I'd got those thirty pages right.

So we met in London, I sat at a desk and read the thirty pages; Lewis didn't interrupt once. I finished the thirty pages and he said to me, 'You're absolutely right, I don't want to know anymore about notes.'

I suppose he'd been nervous because coming from the world of film, Lewis sometimes has a low opinion of the ability of stage writers to write for films. Now I can understand that because there have been many, many instances in film writing of stage writers thinking of themselves as 'literary men' above the medium of film. There were endless examples in the 1930s, when there used to be 'writing factories' in the big studios, of very many celebrated stage writers going from New York, as it usually was from Broadway, to Los Angeles to work as film writers and then sneering at the job of film writing because I think they couldn't do it. Instead of saying, 'This is a medium that is foreign to me. I can't work in it or I don't want to work in it', because the dollars they were being paid were so big they were tempted in one way to stay in a job that they weren't naturally suited for.

Yet at the same time, a human thing, they had to say for the sake of their own dignity, 'Well it's a second rate job anyway, film writing!' Now film writing isn't a second rate job, film writing is just as much of a first class, first rate job as stage writing but not everybody can do both.

As it works out, I can, because I began my writing career writing for the stage and for a visual medium, television, which I don't think is that much different from feature film writing. So I can quite see why Lewis was nervous, because he'd had that experience of stage writers sneering at his craft and also, I suppose, he in his way was a bit down on the ability of stage writers working in film. What convinced him in this thirty page longhand draft was that I was a film writer as well as a stage writer. Therefore we never needed to waste any time sitting around drafting notes.

But when it came to beginning the screenplay of *Shirley Valentine* he again wanted me to go across and spend a week with him. This time he'd moved down to Cannes so at least the weather was better – of course it's not half so attractive as Paris. By this time I knew that he knew that I knew notes were going to be dumped but by this time I also realised that, like many film directors, part of the process which Lewis enjoyed most of all was that time in which the script is being prepared. The story's taking shape, the way that it's going to be presented is taking shape, albeit on paper, yet of course a film director can see that, and at this time he's not got all of the paraphernalia of film making – he's not having to make forty-five decisions every five seconds. So whilst there were no practical reasons for me to go to Cannes there were lots of probably more important social, emotional reasons, and life and writing isn't a purely practical, logical thing – it often involves things like social and emotional reasons, and I understood that by then.

Interviewer: In the theatre you also have a director.

Willy Russell: You do, but the difference between theatre and film is that in theatre everything that everybody does is aimed at supporting and realising the text. The text is absolute king, it is the Bible; in the beginning was the word, and that still is the truth in theatre. In film that's not the case. The writer is one of a whole group of people who are making a contribution. I think it's the single most important contribution, but the director would probably say his is the most important. The hairdresser, I know, would say that hers is the most important and if you don't have the hairstyles right the film will be a failure but it's only one contribution that goes to make this thing called THE FILM. The film itself is God whereas in the theatre the text itself is what is served.

Interviewer: Except that you do have wardrobe and actors, I mean it is a group art in theatre.

Willy Russell: It is a collaborative art in order to serve the text. Film is a collaborative art in which the text collaborates to service and to produce the film.

Interviewer: It's obvious from your answers that your adaptations are approached in the same way as your original play.

Willy Russell: Not in exactly the same way, they can't be in exactly the same way because you've been through the biggest creative moment, when creating the original play. Adaptation doesn't wring as much out of me because I do put on an adapter's hat. I'm originating certain scenes that were not in the original play and I'm restructuring, I'm finding a different means to tell the story. Nevertheless the original creation is there and it is that from which I am working. I don't have to go through the hellfire that I go through in dredging up the original.

Interviewer: You've got your main character in the stage play of *Shirley Valentine*. In fact you've got more than that because Shirley talks about the other characters in the stage play and you've got your plot.

Willy Russell: Yes, the most difficult thing is to make it exciting for yourself as a writer again. You've been everywhere with this material on stage. The excitement for me comes just in finding the way to realise it cinematically rather than theatrically – it's solving the problems of cinema. That's where I take my sustenance from, that's where I look for it when I come to adapt.

Interviewer: Which of your three adaptations from stage to screen was the most difficult to write?

Willy Russell: I don't think of any one of them as being more difficult. Probably because each of them was an adaptation I don't have particularly horrendous memories of any of them. Whereas with each of those plays, *Educating Rita*, *Shirley Valentine* and *Stags and Hens*, which became *Dancin' thru the Dark*, I remember in the writing of all those plays moments where I thought I'd die before I got them finished because they had such huge problems within them.

It wasn't a case of that on the films; there were hiccups and there was, 'how do we solve this problem?' There were terribly difficult things to face, for example in *Educating Rita* where I'd written a play with two characters in a room and because of the concentration of that room there was an intensity which one knew one could not translate to film. On film two characters in a room for two hours is totally boring and would be crippling for the viewer.

Shirley Valentine was a problem because on stage most of what is said, well everything, is reported. So Shirley reports a moment to you and what she reports is true but is not literal truth. So that when she describes the moment where her husband threw his dinner at her she's not actually describing it exactly as it happened, because by this time it is being reported. There's a danger when you move to film, and film is a very, very literal medium, that if you just put that scene on camera it will have a very different effect from the reported version of it in the theatre.

Interviewer: So that's why you had voice overs and voice to camera.

Willy Russell: That's why we heightened the style immediately by having Shirley address the camera. So that we again conveyed the sense of every scene being reported. We didn't go Now/Flashback, Now/Flashback, Now/Flashback because again that can be an irritating device. But I wanted to convey a sense in which the film, up to the second half of it, was reminiscence and reportage. So again we weren't seeing literally how Joe threw the meal at her, we were seeing Shirley's version of that.

Interviewer: Do you have much involvement, as a writer, in the shooting process?

Willy Russell: No, not really because it seems to me that a writer needs to do his job and to do his job well before shooting begins because once shooting begins it's like being at war – it really is the best analogy. Being on location is being at war and you are at war with everything. The elements, your dwindling budget, your locations, things can go wrong minute by minute. Now, as a writer, if you've got a problem, then it's not the best time to tap the director on the shoulder and say, 'Do you think we can re-jig these lines?' He goes, 'So what do we do? You know I've got ninety people standing around all on a payroll that's eating up money faster than the Gulf Crisis – do we stop shooting?'

Occasionally you get to a moment where you will see something and you meet with the director the night before and you will re-jig a scene but often then you'll have a situation where the producers, the film's backers, will come in and say you can't do that: 'We didn't agree to back a film rewritten, we agreed to back this film.' Now if you could bring everybody together and they could see that you weren't drastically altering the picture but you'd actually at the eleventh hour found a more effective way of presenting a scene then that would be all well and good. But the nature of film is such that often the producers are 5,000 miles away.

That's why I say it's more like an army on the march than anything else, so better for the writer to have got his job done and to leave them to it and to just go out and see them occasionally and have a cup of tea with them.

The other point is that it is also too frustrating to be on location because when writing a film I visualise everything. I don't write dialogue on paper in a vacuum, it's not an abstract scene. I see the picture perfectly in my mind. If I had drawing skills I could storyboard for you every moment from a film of mine to show you how I see the shots and the angle of every moment. Now because I think like that I'm inevitably in conflict with any director who is at work on my work. I don't want that to be an open conflict because I want the director to be able to bring his vision to bear on this material.

Interviewer: Why don't you make your own films, direct them yourself?

Willy Russell: Because I've just said to you it's like a war. Who wants to go to war? I would prefer never having to, but perhaps one day I will, I don't know. I might one day risk it and it may be, of course, that the one thing I discover if I do the job myself is that I can't do the job. That the pictures I have in my mind are the wrong pictures for the finished film. Only trying it will tell. I'm not itching to do it, I don't have any ambition to do it but I have a growing curiosity about it.

Interviewer: You haven't written anything for television since your series *One Summer* written ten years ago. Why is this?

Willy Russell: I think the world of television film and drama has changed drastically since I was writing for it. When I first began in TV the TV drama slot was probably the most important forum for contemporary writers. You had loyalty to a play slot – something like *Play for Today* was watched by between 14 and 18 million viewers, and people talked about what was on telly in the play slot last night. It was where most people's theatre took place, albeit often on film. Issues were presented, the whole of the system supported the fact of having this important forum for which the best writers wrote. That started to be eroded until there came a time, really, where it seemed to me that English television moved from this play slot and into mini film making. Most of the studios, for example, had set up their own in-house film companies, and instead of making films and plays that came out of a British tradition of writing in which, as in theatre, the director, the wardrobe, the producer, the cameramen supported the text, it was moved to a position more like film where it was becoming the director's medium in which the text was merely part of a collaborative process that would make a film.

In so doing they tried to make film, and in some cases succeeded, with what

I would call American production values, high definition, high gloss, and in so doing the content, the centre of these pieces and the centrality of this writing started to be eroded. You no longer had a loyalty to the slot either, so you couldn't get 18 million people watching because the companies would not defend that slot say on a Thursday night.

As with all revolutions and changes economics are usually at the root of it. So at about the time that this was becoming apparent, while it was perfectly possible for me to remain working in TV, I was able to begin writing for feature film. So if I was going to have all the problems you face when you're making a feature film why should I have it within the BBC or ITV, when I could actually be making feature films with people who would release the films in America which is where everybody aims *for*?

Interviewer: You have written two stage musicals. Could they be the basis for future films?

Willy Russell: Well, one of them, called *John, Paul, George, Ringo and Bert* (a play I wrote in the early seventies, my first successful stage play), was going to be filmed, but there were objections from Paul McCartney and whilst I was prepared to consider his objections, the film makers weren't interested in considering these objections. They just wanted to get on and make the film and I think they badly antagonised Paul at one point and so he sought to prevent the film, if it were ever made, being shown in America. The problem for the film makers with that is that whilst they could still release the film in Europe and England, the cost of making the film would be prohibitive because without a release in America they would not have a chance of recouping. There is a law of privacy in America which Paul could successfully have used and so the film fell through, although I had written a screenplay.

Subsequently, I was asked by Paul McCartney to write him a screenplay and I wrote a film called *Band on the Run* which has not been filmed. I'm very lucky, most screenwriters tend to write five to ten scripts which are never filmed for every one that is. At one point Christopher Hampton once said that he'd written eleven screenplays, two of which had been made. He probably gets everything produced now. Now I've had two which have not been done. I have another musical, *Blood Brothers,* and I cannot see a time in which it would be filmed because I do not have sufficient faith that we would be able to make it in a way that ultimately I would welcome and would want to see.

Now that was not the case with *Educating Rita*, *Shirley Valentine* or *Dancin' thru the Dark* – they were relatively low budget films, certainly in American terms, and the brutal fact of film making is that the art side of making a film is a very small percentage of what is involved and one of the facts is that the less that a film is costing the more control the director and producer and the writer will have over its final outcome – that was certainly true in the three films I've made so far.

Blood Brothers, by its very nature, being a musical, a notoriously difficult form, the musical film, a notoriously expensive form, would mean a large input from the business side of film making. And with great respect to businessmen and financiers of film, they are not the people who make the best movies. That is best left to the movie makers.

Interviewer: Music is obviously important to you. How important do you think is the music soundtrack to the finished film?

Willy Russell: Oh, you can completely and utterly alter the impact of a scene with the music you put behind it, or if you choose not to put music behind it. I didn't write any of the music for *Educating Rita*. David Henshal wrote the main theme and I thought it was a beautiful composition, a lovely theme, which worked beautifully, it was so sympathetic to the screenplay.

In *Shirley Valentine* I wrote the main theme but apart from plotting it with Lewis I was not directly in control of how the music would be used. Whereas in *Dancin' thru the Dark* I was virtually, I suppose, the producer for the music for that picture. I had a much, much greater input in terms of where and how the music would be used. I spent a lot of time working with the film in a recording studio and being able to try four seconds of something there and muted topline piano under that, and so on. I've also written soundtracks for other writers' work: a TV series, and a film called *Mr Love*. It's something I'd like to do and to explore further but it's not my main job. I'm trying to write a new play, so at the moment, no matter how tempting it might be, I wouldn't accept a commission to write a score for someone else's film. If I'd just finished writing my own new play and someone came along and said they'd like me to write a score for their new film I'd jump at it.

Interviewer: We've talked a lot about the differences between stage and screen. What about the different techniques of film and stage acting, as I know you have done a bit of both?

Willy Russell: There is a danger here that, again, as with writing, there is an historical wariness of film directors for stage acting. Some directors think that a very good stage actor will not be good because he'll be stagey on film. Well, that's not the case (both Rita and Shirley were played by actresses who had initiated those parts very successfully on stage). You say to most good stage actors: 'Look love, you're hitting that a bit hard, you've got a camera that's six inches from you and it's gonna be blown up so it's eleven feet high on the screen', and they will quickly understand that.

On stage, actors and actresses play the whole range of styles. If you're playing in Restoration comedy you are playing *in a very mannered, loud, over the footlights style,* whereas if on the stage you're playing a very intimate moment in a piece of Ibsen or Chekhov, it still has to be pushed over the footlights – but ultimately you're playing the reality and truth of it as intimately as you would do on film. Now a good actor goes into film and plays that intimacy of Chekhov and plays it with the same intensity without having to throw it out to a thousand people on the other side of the footlights. But he still has to project it. It's just a different way of projecting it – in fact down through the lens onto cellulloid and out ultimately into that cinema auditorium.

Interviewer: And finally what advice would you give to aspiring young screenwriters?

Willy Russell: The one piece of concrete advice I could give is try and retain control of your script until the last possible moment and don't go and live in Hollywood! It's very difficult to give generalised advice in that way; if I was talking specifically to a young writer and had the benefit of seeing his script and knowing where he was at, what he was aiming for, I would presume to give personal advice. But knowing that nobody ever takes advice unless it confirms the course of action they were set on anyway I won't give any advice.

Interviewer: Is there a better question with which we could round off this interview?

Willy Russell: No, I don't think it needs to be rounded. We're talking about film and as a film scene does not need to have a beginning, a middle and an end, a film scene can *be* just an end, just a middle or just a beginning – we should leave it like that.

Introduction

The screenwriter

Willy Russell has written numerous screenplays for both the 'small' and the 'big' screen. His original television films, written during the 1970s, include, three (*Lies, Break-In* and *The Boy with the Transistor Radio*) for Schools' television, two (*Death of a Young Man* and *Our Day Out*) for BBC's *Play for Today* slot and one for ITV (*Daughters of Albion*) for whom Russell also wrote the screenplays for the filmed drama serial *One Summer.*

His three feature films were based by him on his plays *Educating Rita* (commissioned by the RSC in 1979 and released as a film by Columbia in 1983), *Shirley Valentine* (commissioned by Liverpool Everyman Theatre in 1986 and released as a film by Paramount in 1989) and his less well known play *Stags and Hens* (commissioned by Liverpool Everyman Theatre in 1978, which became his most recent feature film release *Dancin' thru the Dark*, 1990).

Willy Russell: background and writing

He was born near Liverpool in 1974 and left school at fifteen. He entered the hairdressing profession – at his mother's suggestion – becoming a ladies' hairdresser for six years and eventually managing a shop in Kirkby. Following this he did a variety of jobs, including stacking stockings in the warehouse at Bear Brand and a brief spell in Ford Motors cleaning girders.

He originally began writing as a songwriter, performing in his late teens at folk clubs and concerts and contributing many songs to local radio programmes. By the time he was twenty he decided to become a playwright, at the same point resolving to become a teacher. Within eighteen months of starting work in Liverpool's schools his play-writing had become successful enough to allow him to pursue it full time.

Looking back on the years after he left school Russell himself has written evocatively:

> *For six years I did a job I didn't understand and didn't like. Eventually I even had my own salon and it was there that on slack days I would retire to the back room and try to do the one and only thing I felt I understood, felt that I could do: write.*
>
> *I wrote songs mostly, but tried, as well, to write sketches and poetry, even a book. But I kept getting interrupted by women who, reasonably enough on their part, wanted their hair done. It dawned upon me that if ever I was to become a writer I had first to get myself into the sort of world which allowed for, possibly even encouraged such aspiration. But that would mean a drastic change of course. Could I do it? Could I do something which those around me didn't understand? I would have to break away. People would be puzzled and hurt. I compromised. I sensed that the world in which I would be able to write would be the academic world. Students have long holidays. I'd be able to spend a good part of the year writing and the other part learning to do a job, teaching perhaps, which would pay the rent.*

Willy Russell's early theatre work was first produced at his local Liverpool Everyman Theatre which saw the West End transfer and successful run of his musical *John, Paul, George, Ringo and Bert* (1974) and the beginning of his international reputation. This reputation has been confirmed both on stage and screen by a successful run of work since – his second musical, *Blood Brothers* (1983), was still running in London's West End in 1990, along with the stage version of *Shirley Valentine*. Russell is the only living British dramatist, apart from Alan Ayckbourn (writer of *Absurd Person Singular*), to have appeared for every one of the last five years on the Arts Council listing of Britain's top ten most produced playwrights in subsidised theatres.

His work has been performed on stages and screens throughout the world, and although it is invariably set firmly in Liverpool its themes have proved international – crossing barriers of culture, class and creed. It has frequently been nominated for and received many national and international film and theatre awards. He has also been honoured with an MA from the Open University (1983) and a Doctorate from Liverpool University (1989), despite leaving secondary school with only one 'O' level in English!

Comedy and Willy Russell

The historical roots of comedy and comic writing are worth looking at by way of background to Willy Russell's particular dramatic style.

The eighteenth-century writer Dr Samuel Johnson replied to the question 'What is poetry?' with the words, 'It is much easier to say what it is not. We all *know* what light is; but it is not easy to *tell* what it is.' Comedy is similarly difficult to define accurately and to everyone's satisfaction.

Comedy covers many different forms of humour, not all of which appeal to all of us all of the time. There can be the storyteller who has us quietly smiling; the comedian who tells sick or old jokes which just make us groan; the slapstick sketch which has us aching with laughter or the sharply observed situation comedy where we laugh both *with* and *at* the characters. Our own culture, religion, social background, personality and even mood-of-the-moment determine what makes us find something amusing. A group of students reading *Shirley Valentine* will inevitably include some people who find one scene or joke funny which others will not.

In our own times, therefore, we would probably say that comedy is whatever makes us laugh. Yet what we recognise as comic in the 1990s would not necessarily have appealed to an Elizabethan or nineteenth-century audience. In classical literature a comedy was a play in which the main characters and motive triumphed over adversity. Shakespeare's plays are grouped as Tragedies, Comedies and Histories; and in some of the so-called Comedies many very brutal events happen before Good finally wins over Evil. In *The Merchant of Venice*, for example, we have to witness the slow and painful humiliation of Shylock the Jew before the young lovers can be united and peace is restored on an optimistic note.

If we think of some of the famous comedians of this century – Charlie Chaplin, Laurel and Hardy, Peter Sellers, Morecombe and Wise, John Cleese, Eddie Murphy – there is a sort of 'universality' in their comedy which strikes a common chord ... in us all. But it is often said that inside every clown is a sad person trying to escape, and we know that there is often a strong element of seriousness beneath the surface of great comedy; Charlie Chaplin made a brilliantly funny film called *The Great Dictator* – its subject was Hitler!

A read through two of Willy Russell's early screenplays for television reveals just that thread of seriousness lurking not far beneath the surface comedy. *Our Day Out* (see Wider reading) is a short drama about a school party's day trip to a zoo and then the seaside. It begins in a Liverpool street; Carol is rushing to school, Les is the lollipop man:

LES	*'Ey you!*
CAROL	(Stopping) *What?*
LES	*Come here. Come on!*
CAROL	(Approaching him) *Agh ey, Les. Come on. I wanna get t'school.*
LES	*That makes a bloody change.*
CAROL	*We're goin' out. On a trip.*
LES	*Now listen. Are you listenin'? Y' don't across the road without the assistance of the lollipop man. And that's me!*
CAROL	*There's nott'n comin', though.*
LES	*Now just listen; I know it might look as though there's nothin' comin' but how do you know that a truck or car isn't gonna come speedin' out of that side road? Eh?*
CAROL	(Looking) *Oh yeh. I never thought of that.*
LES	*No. I know y'didn't. Y' never do. None of y'. That's why the government hired me to look after y' all.*
CAROL	*Ta Les.*
LES	*Ey. Where y' goin' today then?*
CAROL	*It's somewhere far away. I forget.*
LES	*They all goin'?*
CAROL	*Only the kids who go to the Progress Class.*
LES	*What's that?*
CAROL	*What? Y' don't know what the Progress Class is? It's Mrs Kay's class. Y' go down there in the week if y' can't do sums or writing. If y' backward like.*
LES	*By Christ, I'll bet she's kept busy. They're all bloody backward round here.*

The quick verbal exchanges between the characters – faithfully presented in the local dialect – run through the entire play; interwoven with the comedy are some trenchant observations about the way young people behave on their day out with the teachers. In particular, the climax of the drama focuses on Carol, depressed about her life to the point of suicide. She looks around at run-down urban Liverpool and desperately wants to escape from its bleak horizons. As one of the teachers says to her: 'Carol ... you're talking as though you've given up on life already. You sound as though life for you is just ending, instead of beginning.'

This theme of escape is taken up in a subsequent play, *The Boy with the Transistor Radio*, in which Russell again shows how adept he is at capturing people who lose out, despite their good intentions, especially those trapped in the inner-city environment of his native Liverpool. The following conversation takes place between a teacher and Terry, the sad anti-hero of the piece who lives in a dream world created by a radio disc jockey:

TERRY   *Sir, I don't half feel sorry for you.*

TEACHER   (Smiling, puzzled) *Why?*

TERRY   *Well, it's like ... you've been tryin' to teach us lot for the last five years, haven't y'? An', like most of us, we're gonna walk out them gates as thick as when we come in, aren't we?*

TEACHER   *Come on ... you've learnt somethin' since you've been here....*

TERRY   *Oh, yeh. But I mean, there's none of us gonna light up the world as far as brains are concerned. But just think, sir, just think that if you'd been a DJ for the last five years – just think how many people would have listened to y' then, an' they would have listened properly. No talkin' at the back or missin' lessons then. Know what I mean, sir?*

TEACHER   *Well ... erm ... er, yes ... I think so....*

TERRY   *Yeh.*

TEACHER   *Terry ... listen ... look.... Radios, the music you listen to, the disc jockeys and the advertising – that sort of thing ... you've got to realize that all that sort of thing is a reflection of a world that is not necessarily accurate. Just because you listen to the radio a lot, Terry, it doesn't mean that you'll live your life in paradise.* (Pause) *I mean, these fellows on the radio station who are telling you that everything's fine, everything's easy and uncomplicated – well, you're not ... you're not meant to believe it.*

While Russell's stock-in-trade of witty one-liners are less evident in this screenplay, what is again apparent is his interest in the dream and reality of 'escape'. It is a compassionate yet painful piece which skilfully explores the gulf between the dreams that are constantly dangled in front of us by the media, and the more mundane realities of everyday life.

In taking stock of Willy Russell's earlier writing for the stage what emerges clearly is an unnerving and subtle mix of enjoyable comedy and serious social message, characteristic of the best dramatists. Russell can be seen as another playwright in the unbroken line from Shakespeare to Bernard Shaw to John Osborne to the present day who succeeds in communicating with an audience in such a fashion that they are at once popularly entertained and compellingly educated.

Educating Rita

The creation of Rita in *Educating Rita* would seem − looking from the outside − to be a logical next step in Russell's development as a writer. Here is a young woman − like Carol and Terry in the earlier stories − having missed out at school, but determined in her late twenties to make something of herself. Thus she attends Open University tutorials and, putting her husband's prejudices and her tedious hairdressing job behind her, goes in search of new horizons. Needless to say, the new path is not without its pitfalls and, in Willy Russell's hands, not without its comic, even absurd moments.

In the following extract Rita is recounting to her tutor Frank one of the highlights of her Open University summer-school:

RITA   *Y' know at first I was dead scared. I didn't know anyone. I was gonna come home. But the first afternoon I was standin' in this library, y' know lookin' at the books, pretendin' I was dead clever. Anyway, this tutor come up to me, he looked at the book in me hand an' he said, 'Ah, are you fond of Ferlinghetti?' It was right on the tip of me tongue to say, 'Only when it's served with Parmesan cheese', but, Frank, I didn't. I held it back an' I heard meself sayin', 'Actually, I'm not too familiar with the American poets'. Frank, you woulda been dead proud of me. He started talkin' to me about the American poets − we sat around for ages − an' he wasn't even one of my official tutors, y' know. We had to go to this big hall for a lecture, there must have been two thousand of us in there. After he'd finished his lecture this professor asked if anyone had a question, an', Frank, I stood up!* (She stands) *Honest to God, I stood up, an' everyone's lookin' at me. I don't know what possessed me, I was gonna sit down again, but two thousand*

> *people had seen me stand up, so I did it, I asked him the question.*
> There is a pause and Frank waits

FRANK *Well?*

RITA *Well what?*

FRANK *What was the question?*

RITA *Oh, I dunno, I forget now, cos after that I was askin' questions all week, y' couldn't keep me down. I think that first question was about Chekhov; cos y' know I'm dead familiar with Chekhov now.*

Rita emphatically achieves her ambitions to be formally educated into the realms of English Literature, only to find that her tutor and mentor Frank does not quite like what he has created. (There are interesting parallels here with Eliza Doolittle and Professor Higgins in Bernard Shaw's play *Pygmalion*.) As *Educating Rita* draws to a close we realise that the playwright has not only been exploring further his preoccupation with escape from 'working-class' roots, but ultimately questioning where such 'escape' then leads. Rita has inevitably grown away from her husband Denny and former friends, finding herself occupying a rather different social milieu. Russell's satire is not spared as Rita rounds on the drunken Frank:

RITA *I'll tell you what you can't bear, Mr Self-Pitying Piss Artist; what you can't bear is that I am educated now. What's up, Frank, don't y' like me now that the little girl's grown up, now that y' can no longer bounce me on daddy's knee an' watch me stare back in wide-eyed wonder at everything he has to say? I'm educated, I've got what you have an' y' don't like it because you'd rather see me as the peasant I once was; you're like the rest of them – you like to keep your natives thick, because that way they still look charming and delightful. I don't need you.* (She gets up and picking up her bag moves away from the desk in the direction of the door) *I've got a room full of books. I know what clothes to wear, what wine to buy, what plays to see, what papers and books to read. I can do without you.*

FRANK *Is that all you wanted. Have you come all this way for so very, very little?*

RITA *Oh it's little to you, isn't it? It's little to you who squanders every opportunity and mocks and takes it for granted.*

FRANK *Found a culture have you, Rita? Found a better song to sing have you? No – you've found a different song, that's all – and on your lips it's shrill and hollow and tuneless. Oh, Rita, Rita ...*

Educating Rita is one of the high points of Willy Russell's work to date. In it he brings to fruition his writing about the social issues of education and equal opportunity — the plot is dotted with autobiographical and local Liverpool detail. But the play is not just the 'message'. Throughout the drama there is a sparkling wit at work, the dialogue bursting with splendidly funny one-liners, quips, jokes and intellectual wordplay that ensure both great enjoyment and a keen sense of pace for any audience.

Shirley Valentine

When the film *Shirley Valentine* opens with Shirley's words, 'Talkin' to a microwave! Wall, what's the world comin' to?', we know at once that here is the Rita-type character, this time forty-something rather than twenty-six, sadly reflecting on her lot as the bored housewife, a life of wasted opportunities littered behind her. Shirley's tale is set in familiar Russell territory, Liverpudlian semi-detached-land where children, friends and neighbours alike are presented living out lives of quiet desperation, punctuated by the odd moment of excitement and glamour.

The first half of the screenplay profiles the contemplative Shirley, reliving moments from schooldays alongside her role as mother to two teenage children. But it is her role as wife to husband Joe which most troubles her, to the point of dreaming of escape — that theme again! Dreams become reality in the shape of her friend Jane; as the second part of the drama opens we find them on holiday in an idyllic Greek isle, far removed from the rainy streets of Liverpool. What ultimately happens to Shirley and Joe? You will need to read the screenplay to discover for yourself.

Thinking back over Willy Russell's dramatic work, on reading *Shirley Valentine* two aspects of his creative energies come shining through. First, there is his obvious indignation at undeveloped potential, in this case in the shape of Shirley. Just as with Rita before her, Shirley is moved to observe:

> *I've lived such a little life. An' even that'll be over pretty soon. I'd allowed myself to live this little life — when inside me there was so much more. An' it's all gone unused. An' now it never will be. Well. Why do we get all this life if we don't ever use it?*

Why do we all get these...feelings and dreams and hopes – if we don't ever use them?

page 61

And, again in common with Rita, Shirley does something – however small and apparently insignificant – about challenging the status quo. She decides to take her life by the scruff of the neck and explore change.

This 'social message' aspect was interestingly commented upon by reviewers of the play when it first came to the London stage, starring actress Pauline Collins in the title role. Irving Wardle wrote:

*Nothing could be more banal than the subject of **Shirley Valentine:** it is the old chestnut of the turning worm. But if you think of its past treatments, they are obsessively worked out either towards defeat or mere wish-fulfilment. The subject has been hijacked by the bourgeois stage to reinforce the status quo.... Mr Russell's characters are not interested in the ultimate defeats of human existence; they are interested in escaping a lousy deal and getting more out of life while there is still time.*

It is certainly a class-conscious message; but it comes from an artist as passionately attached as Bernard Shaw to the idea of personal growth, and it sends you out of the theatre thinking better of the human race.

Later in the same review Wardle concludes:

Neither in the writing nor the playing is there the least trace of revenge. Nor, despite the play's extraordinary occupation of a woman's mind, does the piece rank as an exercise in male feminism.

As a point of comparison, critic Peter Kemp, writing of the same production, noted:

In summary, it sounds a combination of feminist tract and Mills and Boon escapism: the housewife who disentangles herself from the tentacles of domesticity for days of sun-baked dining on fried squid.

The extent to which the screenplay balances its 'messages' and its entertainment value is worth considering as you read it. What is also worth giving some thought to is how successful you think Willy Russell is as a *male* writer trying to see the world from a *female* standpoint.

If *what* the screenplay has to say is one key aspect to be examined, *how* it speaks to us is the second point worth debating. It is instructive in this context to reflect on Russell's origins as a writer – namely, his deep interest in folk songs. For there is much in his style which might remind us of the traditional folk ballad: its underpinning moral, its poetic phrasing, its eye for detail and, above all, its debt to the oral tradition of storytelling. Accomplished comic writing is notoriously difficult; too often, the one-liners of the kind that tumble from Shirley's lips will just make an audience wince. In Russell's hands the dialogue is expertly and tightly crafted, the balance of high comedy and quieter moments skilfully weighed. As theatre critic Michael Coveney wrote:

> These anecdotes are strung together in a sideways-on, buttonholeing, club comic manner. The form is both a theatrical device and a celebration of a quirky conversational idiom.

Playwright Jack Rosenthal once said: 'I believe comedy is the best way to learn the truth about ourselves.' As you read *Shirley Valentine* see whether you find any truth in his statement.

Theatre and cinema

Reading the theatre critics' reviews in the previous section must remind us that *Shirley Valentine* was originally written as a monologue for the stage. But following the great success of the film *Educating Rita* it is no surprise that Willy Russell was asked to write a screenplay version of *Shirley Valentine*, the text of which appears in this edition. As you are reading try to remember both the text's origins and that what you are studying was the source from which the film director worked. The extracts from the stage play on pages 103–4 and 104–5 present fascinating points of comparison for discussion.

That both *Educating Rita* and *Shirley Valentine* have proved so popular with audiences around the world is hardly astonishing. They give us marvellous twentieth-century comedies of manners, with glimpses into Liverpool suburbia, a university campus and a Greek island thrown in for good measure. Willy Russell is quoted as saying:

It wasn't until I started playing the guitar in folk clubs that I found a non-high art form I could really relate to.

Theatre had always seemed a highbrow slap in the face to people like me. I just couldn't relate to any of it either culturally or socially: it didn't seem to be about people like me, and people like me never seemed to go and look at it.

With Rita and Shirley the writer has given both the theatre and the cinema of the 1980s and 1990s the voices of local people, speaking irrepressibly in their home dialect. In twentieth-century history of film and stage critics may well observe in years to come that an interesting step was made from Eliza Doolittle's excruciating vowel sounds, via John Osborne's 'angry young men', to Shirley's 'thy feller will have one big gob on him all night long'.

Reading log

One of the easiest ways of keeping track of your reading is to keep a log book. This can be any exercise book or folder that you have to hand, but make sure you reserve it exclusively for reflecting on your reading, both at home and in school.

As you read the screenplay, stop from time to time and think back over what you have read.

- Is there anything that puzzles you? Note down some questions that you might want to research, discuss with your friends or ask a teacher. Also note any quotations which strike you as important or memorable.

- Does your reading remind you of anything else you have read, heard or seen on TV or at the cinema? Jot down what it is and where the similarities lie.

- Have you had any experiences similar to those narrated in the screenplay? Do you find yourself identifying closely with one or more of the characters? Record this as accurately as you can.

- Do you find yourself really liking, or really loathing, any of the characters? What is it about them that makes you feel so strongly? Make notes that you can add to.

- Can you picture the locations and settings? Draw maps, plans, diagrams, drawings, in fact any doodle that helps you make sense of these things.

- Now and again try to predict what will happen next in the screenplay. Use what you already know of the author, the genre (type of play) and the characters to help you do this. Later record how close you were and whether you were surprised at the outcome.

- Write down any feelings that you have about the screenplay. Your reading log should help you to make sense of your own ideas alongside those of the author.

Shirley Valentine

the Screenplay

Characters

Shirley Valentine

PARAMOUNT PICTURES PRESENTS A
LEWIS GILBERT / WILLY RUSSELL PRODUCTION
SHIRLEY VALENTINE
PAULINE COLLINS TOM CONTI as COSTAS
Music Score by WILLY RUSSELL and GEORGE HADJINASSIOS
Executive Producer JOHN DARK Written by WILLY RUSSELL
Produced and Directed by LEWIS GILBERT A PARAMOUNT PICTURE

The film was released in 1989 with the following cast:

SHIRLEY VALENTINE   *Pauline Collins*
COSTAS   *Tom Conti*
GILLIAN   *Julia McKenzie*
JANE   *Alison Steadman*
MARJORIE   *Joanna Lumley*
HEADMISTRESS   *Sylvia Syms*
JOE   *Bernard Hill*
DOUGIE   *George Costigan*
JEANETTE   *Anna Keaveney*
MILLANDRA   *Tracie Bennett*
SYDNEY   *Ken Sharrock*
THELMA   *Karen Craig*
BRIAN   *Gareth Jefferson*
YOUNG SHIRLEY   *Gillian Kearney*
YOUNG MARJORIE   *Catharine Duncan*
LONDONER   *Cardew Robinson*

LONDONER'S WIFE   *Honora Burke*
RENOS   *Marc Zuber*
SHARON LOUISE   *Deborah Yhip*
EXECUTIVE TYPE   *Ray Armstrong*
GERMAN TOURIST   *John Hartley*
GERMAN TOURIST   *Marlene Morley*
CHAMBERMAID   *Annee Blott*
MALE TEACHER   *Matthew Long*
VERONICA   *Ruth Russell*
MAUREEN   *Sarah Nolan*
LIZ   *Diane Whitley*
CAROL   *Joanne Zorian*
SALLY   *Geraldine Griffiths*
WOMAN IN TAVERNA   *Elaine Boisseau*
SPIRO   *Giorgos Xidakis*
COOKING TEACHER   *Sheila Aza*
KID IN CAR   *Alex Wright*
VAN DRIVER   *Ged McKenna*

Produced and directed by   *Lewis Gilbert*

Shirley Valentine

The film's title track starts under a blue and white drawing of SHIRLEY VALENTINE *ironing.*

MAIN TITLES START.

Series of fifteen more drawings of SHIRLEY VALENTINE *are shown at various domestic activities including cleaning, making beds, gardening and shopping whilst the track continues and as the rest of the main title credits are overlaid.*

Main titles finish but track continues over two final drawings.

A drawing of SHIRLEY VALENTINE *walking towards the camera with bags of shopping.*

Dissolve to:
a drawing of a street of small semi-detached houses with small front gardens.

Dissolve to:

1 *Exterior of street – day*

We see in actuality the street of small semi-detached houses. SHIRLEY VALENTINE *walks into shot. She turns into one of the houses and walks up the path to her front door.*

2 *Interior* SHIRLEY'S *kitchen – day*

SHIRLEY *opens her front door and enters as the title track fades. She closes her front door and walks along the passage into the kitchen. She closes the kitchen door and leans against it, sighing. She puts down her shopping bag on the table and turns away to talk to the wall.*

SHIRLEY   Hello Wall.

She turns and looks towards the CAMERA.

SHIRLEY   Well, what's wrong with that?

She turns and moves away. Takes off her coat, and hangs it on a hook.

SHIRLEY   There's a woman three doors down – talks to her microwave.

She turns to the WALL.

SHIRLEY   Talkin' to a microwave! (*to* WALL) Wall, what's the world comin' to?

She goes to the refrigerator, opens it, takes out a bottle of white wine. She speaks to the CAMERA.

SHIRLEY   I know! I'm wicked, aren't I? Drinkin'.

She shuts the fridge door and uncorks the bottle as she walks towards the table where she pours herself a glass of wine.

SHIRLEY   I like a glass of wine when I'm doin' the cookin' – (*to the* WALL)   Don't I Wall? Don't I like a glass of wine when I'm preparing the evening meal?
SHIRLEY   Chips an' egg.

She crosses to the sink, taking a sip of wine as she goes. She puts her glass down and takes some potatoes from a cupboard. Then switches on the tap.

SHIRLEY   Oh God!

She glances at the wall and pulls a face. To the WALL . . .

SHIRLEY   What will *he* be like, eh Wall? My feller? What will he be like when he finds out he's only gettin' chips an' egg for his tea?

She picks up a knife to peel the potatoes. As she does this, she talks to the CAMERA.

2

SHIRLEY   Well, it's Thursday, y'see. And on Thursday it has to be steak. It's the Eleventh Commandment. Moses declared it. 'Thou shalt give thy feller steak every Thursday. And if thou doesn't, thy feller will have one big gob on him all night long.'

She puts the potatoes and knife in a bowl, picks up her glass, then returns to face the CAMERA.

SHIRLEY   I wouldn't mind. It's not even my bloody fault about the steak. You see this morning Gillian came round.

Flashback

3 *Exterior* SHIRLEY'S *house – day*

SHIRLEY *draws aside her curtains and looks out.*

SHIRLEY (*voice over – VO*)   I don't normally have much to do with Gillian.

From SHIRLEY'S *viewpoint we see Gillian crossing the road from her house to Shirley's house.*

SHIRLEY (*VO*)   I'm not sayin' she's a bragger – but if you've been to Paradise, she's got a season ticket. She's that type, Gillian. You know, if you've got a headache . . . .

4 *Interior* SHIRLEY'S *hall and front door*

We see the silhouette of someone in the frosted glass of SHIRLEY'S *front door. She moves back and lets the curtains fall. We hear the sound of the front door knocker.* SHIRLEY *moves to the front room door.*

SHIRLEY (*VO*)   . . . . she's got a brain tumour.

SHIRLEY *moves to the front door and opens it.* GILLIAN *is outside, beaming.*

GILLIAN   Oh, hello, Shirley. It appears that your bell isn't working. Do you think perhaps there's something wrong with it?

GILLIAN *steps forward and presses the bell.*
SHIRLEY (*VO*) That's how she talks – Gillian. Y'know – she begrudges you the breath.

SHIRLEY *turns* to GILLIAN.

SHIRLEY I don't know. There must be a power cut.
GILLIAN Ah, well, there you see. Eric and I have installed solar energy. Now we would never be caught out by a power failure.

GILLIAN *speaks to* SHIRLEY *in the doorway.*

GILLIAN Shirley, I've come to ask for a favour. Can you come round for a minute?
SHIRLEY Oh yeah, Yeah, sure.

She steps out of the house, pulling the front door shut behind her. As they move out into the street and cross the road, GILLIAN *continues talking.*

GILLIAN You see, Eric and I have to go away for a couple of days. Eric's giving a paper in Brussels. Bloody Brussels! I said to him, why couldn't it have been Paris – or even Amsterdam? I really find Brussels such a bore.

As they walk to GILLIAN's *front gate and up her path to the front door.*

SHIRLEY Yeh, it must be. All those sprouts.

GILLIAN *leads the way into the house.*

GILLIAN I'd made arrangements for Mummy to feed Claymore – but she finds now she can't do this evening. So if you *could* manage . . .

5 Interior GILLIAN'S **kitchen – day**

A very modern, fitted kitchen. In a corner, a large sad-eyed bloodhound – CLAYMORE – lies in his basket. GILLIAN *enters, followed by* SHIRLEY.

GILLIAN (*off*)   Now, we keep Claymore's food in here.

She takes out a box of muesli and puts it beside the sink, next to CLAYMORE'S *bowl.*

GILLIAN   Now, it's terribly simple, Shirley. You simply mix his muesli with about half a pint . . .
SHIRLEY (*disbelievingly*) Doesn't he have meat?

GILLIAN *laughs as she puts some muesli into the bowl and pours milk on to it.*

GILLIAN   Oh, Shirley! We haven't had meat in this house for years. Didn't you know we'd become vegans?
SHIRLEY   No, I thought you were still Church of England.

GILLIAN *takes the bowl and, crouching down, puts it in front of* CLAYMORE.

GILLIAN   Now, it's one bowl, Shirley – one bowl twice a day. Claymore loves his muesli . . . (*to* CLAYMORE) . . . don't you, Clay, darling?

CLAYMORE *in his basket whines.*

SHIRLEY   A vegetarian bloodhound!

CLAYMORE *stares at the muesli, then up at* GILLIAN *with mournful eyes. He gets out of his basket and goes to his bowl. He whines.*

GILLIAN (*coaxingly*) Come on, that's it Claymore darling – There. Oh Claymore, darling – it's your favourite.

She stirs the muesli with a finger. CLAYMORE *sniffs at the muesli unenthusiastically. He looks at* GILLIAN.

GILLIAN   I hope you're not sick.

SHIRLEY *stands looking down sympathetically at* CLAYMORE. *We hear* SHIRLEY.

SHIRLEY (*VO*)   You only had to take one look at that dog to see it was well an' truly sick. Sick of the sight of muesli.

CLAYMORE *turns his head away and whines.*

GILLIAN Oh you're off your food because Mummy was five minutes late with it. Is that what it is?

She strokes CLAYMORE'S *face.* SHIRLEY *looks down at them.*

GILLIAN He wants dinner sharp at ten past five and then he has a run in the garden.

SHIRLEY *nods resignedly.*

6 *Exterior street and* GILLIAN'S *house – city suburbs – day*

SHIRLEY *comes hurrying along, carrying a full shopping basket. She pushes open* GILLIAN'S *gate and walks up the path to the house.*

7 *Interior* GILLIAN'S *kitchen – day*

SHIRLEY *is on her knees on the floor, trying to persuade* CLAYMORE *to eat the bowl of muesli she has mixed for him. On the kitchen table is her basket of shopping.* CLAYMORE *sits looking at the muesli without interest.*

SHIRLEY (*pleadingly*) Come on Clay. Go on – Oh look, lovely dinner. It's lovely dinner.

CLAYMORE *lifts his head and looks at her forlornly, with a small piteous whine.*

SHIRLEY There's a lovely dinner. Come on eat it up. Come on Clay – come on (SHIRLEY *sits back on her heels*). Oh, it's not natural, is it? I mean, if God had wanted to create a vegetarian dog, he wouldn't have made you a bloodhound would he? He would have made you a yogurt hound – or a nut rissole hound. But you're a bloodhound. You need meat. Wait 'til you see what I've got for you.

She takes a packet from her shopping basket and opens it, revealing a large rump steak. She takes a knife from a drawer. CLAYMORE *sits up, his nose twitching with interest.* SHIRLEY *starts cutting the steak into chunks, putting them in* CLAYMORE'S *bowl.*

SHIRLEY Oh what's this? Hm. Oh, you wait 'til you taste this Clay – nice dinner. I bet you've never tasted anything like this.

She finishes cutting up the steak, takes a bowl, kneels on the floor and puts it in front of CLAYMORE. *He attacks it with gusto.*

SHIRLEY You get your chops round this. Come on Clay. It's your birthday. . . . Go on. Hmm . . . that's lovely. Greedy Guts, that's Joe's tea you're guzzlin'.

End of flashback

8 *Interior* SHIRLEY'S *kitchen – day*

SHIRLEY *is peeling potatoes at the sink. As she works, she speaks to the* CAMERA.

SHIRLEY I think chips an' egg is nice for a change don't *you?* Mind you, I don't think Joe'll see it quite like that. Oh, sod it – have another glass of wine, Shirley.

She picks up the bottle of wine and refills her glass, speaking to the CAMERA.

SHIRLEY I never used to drink wine. It was our Millandra who started me on this. She said to me, she said . . .

Flashback

9 *Interior wine bar – day*

SHIRLEY *walks in with* MILLANDRA *and* SHARON LOUISE.

MILLANDRA Everybody drinks wine now.
SHIRLEY But I like rum and coke.
MILLANDRA For God's sake! Rum an' coke went out with the Ark, didn't it, Sharon Louise?
SHARON LOUISE Hmm.

MILLANDRA   Anyway, they don't sell rum an' coke here – it's a wine bar. Look – they sell wine.

SHIRLEY   Oh, just wine?

MILLANDRA   Oh, for God's sake . . .

SHARON LOUISE   But there are thousands of different varieties of wine, Mrs Bradshaw. I like Alsatian wine.

SHIRLEY *is now sitting at the table.*

MILLANDRA   And that's what we're going to have.

SHIRLEY *(VO)*   Kids! They know everything, don't they?

MILLANDRA *and* SHARON LOUISE *are now at the bar.*

SHIRLEY *(VO)*   Our Millandra shares a flat with Sharon Louise.

End of flashback

10 *Interior SHIRLEY'S kitchen – day*

SHIRLEY *is still chipping the potatoes. She speaks to the* CAMERA.

SHIRLEY   They're fascinated by sex. Well, I suppose I'd have been the same if I'd been born into their generation. Because they discovered it, y'see – the clitoris. The Clitoris Kids, I call them. And good luck to them. Don't begrudge them a thing. Mind you it was different in my day.

Flashback

11 *Interior lounge bar – public house – night*

The bar is reasonably busy. There is music from loud-speakers. In a corner, round a table, sit SHIRLEY *– at this time she is only about thirty years old – and three other women of about the same age –* LIZ, CAROL *and* SALLY. *They have drinks in front of them. They are all laughing uproariously.*

SHIRLEY   D'you know . . . . D'you know when *I* was a girl I'd
never even *heard* of the clitoris.

LIZ   No-one had. In those days, everyone thought it was just a
case of in out, in out, shake it all about, stars would light up
the sky an' the earth would tremble.

They all laugh.

CAROL   Hey the only thing that trembled for *me* was the
headboard on the bed.

More laughter.

SHIRLEY   When *I* first read about it, I thought it was
pronounced cli*tor*is.

SALLY   I think it sounds nicer that way.

SHIRLEY   That way it sounds like it could be a name . . .

SALLY   It's nicer that way.

SHIRLEY   'Oh, hiya, Cli*tor*is, how are you?'

More laughter.

SALLY   That makes it sound a bit – crude, somehow.

ALL   Oh!

SHIRLEY   Oh shut up! Why not? Plenty of men walkin' round
called Dick.

Laughter again.

SHIRLEY   Well anyway that's the way I thought it was pronounced when I first mentioned it to Joe – you know sitting
in the front room one night. I said, 'Joe' I said 'have you
ever heard of the cli*tor*is?' He didn't even look up from his
paper. 'Yeh', he said. 'But it doesn't go as well as the Ford
Cortina.'

A scream of laughter from the others.

End of flashback

12 *Interior* SHIRLEY'S *kitchen – day*

SHIRLEY *is finishing chipping the potatoes. She speaks to the* CAMERA, *smiling.*

SHIRLEY   Ah they were great, those mates. I don't see them any more. Ah well, that's the way it goes. And now Millandra's gone – and our Brian's left home as well.

Flashback

13 *Exterior maisonette block – day*

A grey day, a drizzle of rain. The maisonettes are in a suburban slum. The building is near-derelict. Peeling plaster, boarded-up windows, a weed-infested front garden. Standing looking at it are SHIRLEY *and* BRIAN. *As they move we hear* SHIRLEY.

SHIRLEY *(VO)*   He's livin' in a squat now. In Kirkby. It's like Beirut on a bad day.

BRIAN *turns to* SHIRLEY *with a proud, beaming smile.*

BRIAN   D'you like it, Mam?

SHIRLEY *stops walking and turns to face* BRIAN.

SHIRLEY   Well, it's – er – got that lived-in look, hasn't it?
BRIAN   We're gonna plant flowers.
SHIRLEY   Ah Son.

They start to walk again.

SHIRLEY   If you're goin' to live in a squat . . . I mean, it's nice here, but . . . well, couldn't you pick somewhere nice you know? Somewhere like Woolton – or Childwall?
BRIAN *(patiently)*   Mother, Childwall is no place for a poet.

He smiles proudly.

SHIRLEY   A what?

BRIAN   A poet, Mam. I've become a poet. I went down the job centre today, an' I signed on – as a poet. Britain's first ever busker poet.

SHIRLEY   Is there much call for that sort of thing round here?

BRIAN   Watch.

He walks across to two KIDS *sitting in front seats of a car. He stops and bends down to them.*

BRIAN *(chanting)*   'Don't rob cars, it's mad, it's bad.
   Think of your Ma's, it'd make them sad.'

BRIAN *looks at* SHIRLEY *then back at the kids.*

BRIAN   'Your Mothers would get a broken heart,
   If you got smashed up, get wise, get
   smart; Don't . . . rob . . . cars.'

The two KIDS *shout simultaneously.*

KID *(in driving seat)*   Piss off!

The car jerks forward. BRIAN *jumps clear as it speeds off with a scream of tyres and a cloud of dust.* BRIAN *comes back to* SHIRLEY.

BRIAN   Poets have always had a hard time of it.

SHIRLEY *nods sympathetically and they walk away arms round each other.*

End of flashback

14 *Interior* SHIRLEY'S **kitchen – day**

SHIRLEY *has the chipped potatoes on a cloth and is carefully drying them off. As she works, she talks, sometimes to the* CAMERA, *sometimes to the* WALL.

SHIRLEY *(reminiscently)*   I do miss them, the kids. Don't I, Wall? There's only me an' him now . . . What's he like? My feller? What's he like, eh Wall? Well, he walked in one night with a smile on his face an' we didn't recognise him. Thought we had a lodger didn't we? He used to laugh, Joe. We both did. Hey, Wall you remember when we first moved in here?

As she continues speaking . . .

Flashback

15 *Interior SHIRLEY'S kitchen, 1965 – day*

SHIRLEY *and* JOE *are newly married in their young twenties. Both in overalls, they are happily painting the kitchen with lemon emulsion using wide brushes. He is on a pair of steps.*

SHIRLEY (*VO*) Oh that seems a long time ago. We hadn't long been married . . .

As JOE *works, he accidentally flicks some paint from his brush. It splashes across her face.*

SHIRLEY Hey.

JOE *stops painting the wall and turns round to look at* SHIRLEY.

JOE What?

SHIRLEY (*from up the ladder*) I can do my own make-up, thank you very much.

JOE *looks at his paint brush.*

JOE (*laughing*) Oh sorry, well it's only a speck. You're bound to get a bit o' paint on you doin' a job like this, aren't you?

He resumes painting. SHIRLEY *dips her brush in her can of paint and flicks it up at* JOE. *It hits the side of his face. He turns.*

JOE Hey!

She has resumed her painting. She turns to him innocently.

SHIRLEY What?
JOE You did that on purpose, didn't you?

SHIRLEY What?

JOE (*grinning*) You little bugger! Did this!

SHIRLEY No!

He flicks his brush at her. Her face is splattered with paint. He laughs at her. She dips her brush in her can of paint.

JOE (*alarmed*) No . . . Shirley. Stop!

She whacks a big dollop of paint at him. SHIRLEY *smiles at him.*

JOE (*screaming*) You bugger!

He turns, puts his brush down, picks up a big brush and holds it up.

JOE Ta.

He bends down to the paint pot. SHIRLEY *is watching him.*

SHIRLEY No, don't.

JOE *holds up a large brush filled with paint.*

JOE I'll get you!

He moves forward.

SHIRLEY (*screams*) No!

As JOE *walks towards* SHIRLEY *she flicks her paint brush at him, he retaliates. She screams and moving to a paint pot by the window, dips her brush in it and turns to* JOE *as he stands laughing by her steps. She flicks the brush at him, he retaliates then backs away.*

SHIRLEY Here, Van Gogh.

She paints JOE *whilst he laughs.*

JOE This is for you, Moaning Lisa.

He flicks his brush at her and covers her with paint. She screams, dips her brush in paint again, flicks it out, then backs away screaming as JOE *moves underneath the steps and points his brush at her.*

SHIRLEY No.

JOE *moves towards her holding up his paint brush.*

SHIRLEY   Don't . . . don't . . . . Oh no, don't Joe. Oh don't.
Please.

Cornered, she covers her head with her arms as JOE *lifts his brush full of
paint. But, instead of painting* SHIRLEY, *he slams the brush over his own
head, down his face and overalls.* SHIRLEY *stares at him in amazement.*

SHIRLEY   You're a bloody headcase! You . . . you are loop the
loop!

JOE *moves in on her, his lips pouting through the paint.*

SHIRLEY (*screaming and laughing*)   Nay I'm not kissin' you like
that!

He makes kissing noises.

JOE   Go on!
SHIRLEY   Nay, all right.

She leans forward and kisses JOE, *rubbing her face against his, smearing
the wet paint over her own face and his.*

16 *Interior* SHIRLEY'S *bathroom, 1965 – day*

SHIRLEY *is sitting in the bath with* JOE *on her lap, leaning back against
her. She is shampooing his hair.*

SHIRLEY   Aren't we the darin' young things, gettin' in the bath
together? Does this mean we're perverted?
JOE (*laughing*)   You're a nutcase, you are.

She leans forward and they kiss.

JOE   I love you . . . Shirley Valentine.

She puts her head against his.

End of flashback

17 *Interior SHIRLEY'S kitchen – day*

SHIRLEY *is standing at the table with a glass of wine in her hand.*

SHIRLEY   Remember that, Wall? He used to *love* me because I was a nutcase. Now he just thinks I *am* a nutcase.

She drinks some wine and addresses the WALL.

SHIRLEY   It's lovely that. It's not too dry. Some of it'd strip the palate off you, wouldn't it? But this is lovely. Do you know what I'd like to do, Wall? I'd like to drink a glass of wine in a country where the grape is grown. Sittin' by the sea just sippin' wine and watchin' the sun go down.

JOE *appears in the open doorway arms folded.*

JOE   What's going on here?

SHIRLEY *swings round to him.*

JOE   Who the bloody hell are you talkin' to?
SHIRLEY   To the wall.

SHIRLEY *picks up a basket of uncooked chips and crosses to the stove. She puts the basket on the stove and alters the controls.*

JOE   To the *what*?
SHIRLEY   The wall. Any objections?

JOE *walks slowly into the kitchen.*

JOE   Never mind the bleedin' wall. It's nearly six o'clock, get on with gettin' me tea.
SHIRLEY   (*hamming it*)   Oh, my God! It's six o'clock and his tea isn't ready. Will the Government collapse? Does this mean the end of civilisation as we know it?
JOE   I always have me tea at six o'clock.
SHIRLEY   So just think how excitin' it would be if for once you had your tea at quarter past six. It'd make the headlines: 'World Exclusive. Joe Eats Late!'

JOE (*glaring at her*) I think you . . . are goin' round the bend.
SHIRLEY Oh, I do hope so. I've always wanted to travel.
JOE Now, listen . . .

SHIRLEY *moves across the kitchen, picks up some bread and walks to the table.*

SHIRLEY No, *you* listen. Go and get a wash and then sit and watch the telly.
JOE Now listen.

SHIRLEY *looks towards* JOE *as she undoes the packet of bread.*

SHIRLEY You'll have your tea when it's ready.

JOE *turns and walks away into the hall. He takes off his coat and scarf.* SHIRLEY *speaks to the* CAMERA.

SHIRLEY I always said I'd leave him when the kids grew up. But by the time they'd grown up there was nowhere to go. I'm not saying he's bad, my feller. He's just no bleedin' good.

She walks away to stove.

SHIRLEY I don't hate men.

She reaches up to the top of the stove, lifts down the basket of chips and holds them over the pan of boiling oil.

SHIRLEY I'm not a feminist. Not like Jane. Jane's me mate.

She puts the basket of chips into boiling oil then looks towards the CAMERA.

SHIRLEY I was havin' tea with her in the café the other day.

Flashback

18 *Interior café – day*

A serve-yourself café in the city centre. SHIRLEY *and* JANE *are sitting at a table. On the table is a tray with a pot of tea, milk, cups and saucers,*

plates and a couple of cakes. JANE *is setting out the cups and saucers.
Over a close shot of* JANE, *we hear:*

SHIRLEY (*VO*) Now, Jane *is* a feminist. Well – she likes to *think*
she is. She reads *Cosmopolitan* and says.
JANE All men are potential rapists.
SHIRLEY Even the Pope?
JANE Of course. All men, without exception.

She nods her head across the café.

JANE Look.

SHIRLEY *turns her head to look. From her viewpoint we see an innocent-
looking man sitting alone at a table across from them, looking around him
casually.* SHIRLEY, *puzzled, turns back to* JANE.

SHIRLEY What?
JANE (*jerking her head*) Him.

SHIRLEY *looks again. Then . . .*

SHIRLEY What about him?
JANE (*leaning forward confidentially*) Since we arrived, he hasn't
taken his eyes off us. He's spent the whole time undressing
us.
SHIRLEY (*wide-eyed*) Go'way! Good job I put my clean underwear on.

She stirs the tea in the pot. In a close shot of JANE, *we see her looking
around the café. Over this we hear:*

SHIRLEY (*VO*) Jane divorced her husband. I never knew him.
It was before I met her. Apparently, she came home from
work unexpectedly one morning and found him in bed – with
the milkman. Honest to God! The milkman! Well, from that
day forward I've noticed she never takes milk in her tea.

In a shot of them both, we see that SHIRLEY *is about to pour milk into
one of the cups, but* JANE *puts her hand over it to stop her. She pulls the
cup of tea in front of her. Then . . .*

JANE   Shirley listen . . . I went in for a magazine competition
and I won it! A fortnight's holiday for two in Greece! How
about that?

SHIRLEY   Jane, what am I going to do without you for a fortnight? You're the only one I *ever* talk to. I won't half miss you.

JANE   No, you won't. 'Cos you're coming with me.

SHIRLEY   What?

JANE   I've got it all fixed. Tomorrow morning we go to the
travel agents and pick the tickets up.

SHIRLEY   Oh, but Jane – I can't.

JANE   Yes, you can. And I don't want a vote of thanks or a
speech about how grateful you are. You'll be doing me a big
favour by coming with me.

19 *Exterior shopping street outside travel agents – day*

JANE *and* SHIRLEY *are coming out of the travel agents.* SHIRLEY *puts a
poster away in her basket. They stop and* JANE *looks at folders and tickets.
She hands a set to* SHIRLEY.

JANE   All set – Tuesday week and we're off.

They walk forward along the street.

JANE   I don't suppose you've got a passport, have you?

SHIRLEY   No. But Jane . . . I . . .

JANE   Come on.

She starts walking quickly along the street. SHIRLEY *hurries after her.*

SHIRLEY   But Jane what about Joe? Jane – it's impossible.

20 *Exterior concourse, main line station – day*

JANE *is walking across the concourse with* SHIRLEY *on her heels.*

JANE   Of *course* it's possible – it's perfectly possible. Just forget
about Joe. You're married to him – not joined at the hip. Has
he ever taken you abroad?

SHIRLEY   No he . . . he'd never go abroad. He hates travellin'.

They stop outside a photo booth.

SHIRLEY   He gets culture shock when we go to Chester!
JANE   Well, that's all right then. Because he's *not* going and you *are*.

JANE *pulls curtain of photo booth aside, pushes* SHIRLEY *in and closes the curtains.*

21 *Interior photo booth – day*

SHIRLEY *is seated facing the camera, posing with a bright smile. The camera flashes.* SHIRLEY *turns to speak through the curtain to* JANE.

SHIRLEY   Do you know if I told Joe I was going to Greece for a week, he'd think I was going for the sex.

As she turns to the camera, it flashes, catching her unprepared. She 'tuts' with irritation, then puts on a fixed grin. JANE'S *voice comes from outside.*

JANE (*VO*)   Well, let him.
SHIRLEY (*still grinning*)   *I* wouldn't mind. I'm not particularly fond of it – sex.

The camera flashes. SHIRLEY *speaks to* JANE *outside.*

SHIRLEY   I think sex is like supermarkets. You know – over-rated.

She smiles archly at the camera. At once, it flashes.

SHIRLEY   It's just a lot of pushin' and shovin' and you still come out with very little at the end.

An even more artificial grin. The camera flashes. SHIRLEY *pulls the curtain aside.*

22 *Exterior concourse, main line station – day*

JANE *is waiting.* SHIRLEY *steps from the booth.*

19

JANE   You get 'em out here. Couple of minutes.

SHIRLEY   Listen Jane – what about Joe?

JANE   Look Shirley, if Joe doesn't want to go abroad – if he wants to behave like every other boring insular Englishman, then that's his prerogative. But you do want to go abroad – you've said so on many occasions. And now you can. That's *your* prerogative. It's no problem, Shirley – it's perfectly logical.

SHIRLEY   I know it's logical – it's dead logical. But you can't bring logic into this. We're talkin' about marriage. Marriage is like the Middle East. There's no solution.

With a whirr, the photo machine delivers a strip of four passport-size photos of SHIRLEY *into a slot.* SHIRLEY *collects them and looks at them. Insert – a quick* CLOSE SHOT *of the photos showing* SHIRLEY *with a glazed, demented grin.*

SHIRLEY   Oh God – I look like the back end of a tram smash!

JANE   Right.

JANE *takes the photos from her, shakes them to dry them.*

JANE   Now then – come on. Bikini.

She starts to walk away. SHIRLEY *goes with her.*

SHIRLEY   Bikini? With my stretch marks? I'd get arrested for bringin' the human form into disrepute.

JANE   Oh, get away!

SHIRLEY   Listen Jane. How am I going to tell Joe that I'm off to Greece for a fortnight?

End of flashback

23 *Interior* SHIRLEY'S *kitchen – day*

SHIRLEY *is standing at the table talking to an imaginary Joe.*

SHIRLEY   Oh, by the way, Joseph – I'm, I'm just poppin' off to Greece for a fortnight . . . (*she walks to the refrigerator*) Yes, yes, I . . . I just thought I'd mention it, so's you could put it down in your diary. (*she takes out a can of lager and puts it on the table*) You won't mind doin' your own washin' an' cookin' for a couple of weeks, will you, doll? . . . There's nothin' to it, babe. (*pointing*) The brown blob on the right of the kitchen is the washin' machine – and the white blob on the left is the cooker. And don't get 'em mixed up, or you might end up with socks on toast!

She lowers her hand despairingly and talks to the WALL.

SHIRLEY   Some chance, eh, Wall? Some chance. Jesus, if I go to the bathroom for five minutes he thinks I've been hijacked.

Door opens and JOE *puts his head round the door.*

JOE   Still here then are we? Haven't forgotten me then eh?
SHIRLEY   It won't be long now.

JOE *disappears closing the door behind him.* SHIRLEY *speaks to the* CAMERA.

SHIRLEY   See what I mean?

She goes to a tall cupboard, pulls the door open and takes out two side plates. We see that on the back of the cupboard door she has pinned the Greek poster she got from the travel agents. She stares at it for a long moment, then takes a jar of pickles off the shelf and closes the door.

SHIRLEY   Oh, I never should have taken the bloody tickets in the first place.

She grimaces and looks across at the WALL.

SHIRLEY   I'll phone Jane tomorrow. She'll easy find someone else to go with her.

She moves back to the table, talking to the CAMERA.

SHIRLEY   And there was me when I was a girl – the only thing I ever wanted was to travel. I always wanted to be an air hostess – or a courier.

As she continues speaking . . .

Flashback

24 *Interior assembly hall, school – day*

The school is assembled, sitting in serried ranks. Open on a CLOSE SHOT *of the fourteen-year-old* SHIRLEY. *Over this we hear the adult* SHIRLEY *as we track back to reveal* MARJORIE MAJORS, *another fourteen-year-old, sitting behind her.*

SHIRLEY (*VO*)   But it was only the clever ones who got to do things like that. The ones like Marjorie Majors. I used to sit next to her in class.

Now in a FULL SHOT, *we see the school assembled, with the* STAFF *on the platform at one end of the hall. The* HEADMISTRESS *is centre stage.*

HEADMISTRESS   Marjorie?
MARJORIE (*in a carefully elocuted voice*)   Miss, although it's often assumed that Niagara Falls are the highest, I think, in fact, it's actually the Angel Falls.

We hear SHIRLEY'S *voice overlaid.*

SHIRLEY (*VO*)   Marjorie took private elocution lessons.
HEADMISTRESS   Can you tell me in what country we would find the Angel Falls?
MARJORIE   Venezuela, Miss.
HEADMISTRESS   Excellent. Twenty-five house points.

MARJORIE *looks smug.*

YOUNG SHIRLEY (*to* CAMERA)   That makes four billion house points she's got so far.

HEADMISTRESS And let us address ourselves to my next question. What was man's most important invention?

In a CLOSE SHOT *we see the sudden shock of delight on* YOUNG SHIRLEY'S *face. Her hand goes up eagerly. Other kids' hands go up, too, including* MARJORIE'S.

HEADMISTRESS (*impatiently*) Oh, Shirley, do put your hand down. You couldn't possibly know the answer.
YOUNG SHIRLEY But Miss . . .

But already the HEADMISTRESS *is pointing to another girl.*

HEADMISTRESS Lorraine?
KID NO. 1 The Sputnik, Miss?
HEADMISTRESS No.

She points at another kid. YOUNG SHIRLEY *waves her hand desperately.*

KID NO. 2 It's the Hoover Miss.
HEADMISTRESS No.

We hear SHIRLEY'S *voice overlaid.*

SHIRLEY (*VO*) But I knew *I* had the *right* answer . . .

The HEADMISTRESS *is pointing.* YOUNG SHIRLEY'S *hand is still up.*

KID NO. 3 Is it the automatic washin' machine Miss?
HEADMISTRESS No.
SHIRLEY (*VO*) . . . 'Cos I'd got it from me dad . . .
KID NO. 4 The aeroplane, Miss?
HEADMISTRESS No.
SHIRLEY (*VO*) . . . And he'd got it from the Encyclopaedia Britannica.

From her viewpoint we see that now only YOUNG SHIRLEY'S *and* MARJORIE'S *hands are up.* YOUNG SHIRLEY'S *arm is aching, but she holds it aloft with her other hand.*

HEADMISTRESS Well come along Marjorie.
MARJORIE (*confidently*) The internal combustion engine, Miss.

As she lowers her hand, we see the triumph on YOUNG SHIRLEY'S *face.*

HEADMISTRESS (*a moment – then*)   No, Marjorie.

YOUNG SHIRLEY (*waving her hand desperately*)   Miss.

Over this we hear SHIRLEY.

SHIRLEY (*VO*)   I was nearly wettin' meself.

YOUNG SHIRLEY   Miss.

SHIRLEY (*VO*)   Knowin' I was on the point of receiving forty three thousand house points, a blessin' from the Pope and the OBE thrown in.

HEADMISTRESS (*with exaggerated toleration*)   Oh, very well Shirley. You might as well get it wrong along with everybody else. What was man's most important invention?

YOUNG SHIRLEY   Miss . . . it was – the wheel!

The other kids all start laughing, nudging each other. The HEADMISTRESS *stares at* YOUNG SHIRLEY *stonily.*

YOUNG SHIRLEY (*louder*)   Miss, it was the wheel! Man's most important invention was the wheel.

Suddenly, the HEADMISTRESS *explodes with rage, pointing a shaking finger at* YOUNG SHIRLEY.

HEADMISTRESS   Somebody must have *told* you!

YOUNG SHIRLEY (*shouting back*)   Well, how the bleedin' hell else could I learn it!

HEADMISTRESS   Be quiet!

YOUNG SHIRLEY   But, Miss, it's not fair!

HEADMISTRESS   Miss Lloyd – the hymn!

MISS LLOYD, *at the piano at the side of the platform, hammers out the opening chords of the hymn. The* HEADMISTRESS *leads the school singing. Over this, we hear* SHIRLEY.

SHIRLEY (*VO*)   And all me house points and me blessin' from the Pope just disappeared before my eyes. I was never really interested in school after that. I became a rebel.

25 *Exterior playground, school – day*

YOUNG SHIRLEY, MAUREEN *and* VERONICA *cross the crowded play-ground – chewing gum and exuding boredom.*

SHIRLEY (*VO*) I used to wear me school skirt so high you would've thought it was a serviette.

The three girls stop behind a corner of the school.

SHIRLEY (*VO*) I was marvellous.

MAUREEN *watches as* VERONICA *lights* YOUNG SHIRLEY'S *cigarette.*

SHIRLEY (*VO*) I used to exude boredom out of every pore. An' I hated everythin'.

YOUNG SHIRLEY *looks round corner then at* VERONICA.

VERONICA What did you have last lesson?
YOUNG SHIRLEY Science.
VERONICA It's garbage – Science.
YOUNG SHIRLEY It's borin'.
MAUREEN What did you do in it?
YOUNG SHIRLEY She showed us this film of these rabbits. Havin' a screw.
VERONICA Any good?
YOUNG SHIRLEY Super – borin'. I don't even like them in stew.
VERONICA I hate them – rabbits.
YOUNG SHIRLEY I hate the world. I hate everythin'. It's all garbage. It's last. It's crap and I hate it.

She peeps round the corner of the wall again, then signals to the others to keep back. YOUNG SHIRLEY *peeps again. From her viewpoint we see, at the other end of the building, a* TEACHER *on playground duty, cup of tea in her hand, walking slowly with* MARJORIE.
Over this we hear SHIRLEY.

SHIRLEY (*VO*) But I didn't really hate anything. The only thing I hated was me.

From YOUNG SHIRLEY'S *point of view we see* MARJORIE *appear again at the other end of the building, alone now. She stands watching them.*

YOUNG SHIRLEY Hi!

YOUNG SHIRLEY *holds up her cigarette and calls to* MARJORIE.

YOUNG SHIRLEY D'you wanna drag?

MARJORIE *disappears behind the building.*

VERONICA D'you think she'll tell?

YOUNG SHIRLEY *shrugs and drags on her cigarette.*

MAUREEN She's a cow. She gives me the irrits.

A TEACHER *appears round the opposite corner of the building and calls sharply.*

TEACHER Shirley Valentine!

YOUNG SHIRLEY *takes the cigarette from her lips as he strides towards them.*

26 *Interior domestic science classroom, school – day*

The class of fourteen-year-old GIRLS *are engaged on a cookery class, supervised by a* MIDDLE-AGED TEACHER. *The* CAMERA *moves in to a* CLOSE SHOT *of* YOUNG SHIRLEY *standing at a table. In front of her is a soufflé, hopelessly sunk. As she stares glumly at it,* MARJORIE *comes to her side and puts her soufflé on the table, beside* YOUNG SHIRLEY'S. *It has risen perfectly. She whispers to* YOUNG SHIRLEY.

MARJORIE Shirley, I *didn't* give you away – honestly. But you *shouldn't* smoke. Smoking can damage your health.

YOUNG SHIRLEY *picks up a pointed knife.*

YOUNG SHIRLEY And I can damage *your* health!

She sticks the knife into MARJORIE'S *soufflé . It collapses before our eyes.*

MARJORIE *looks at it, biting her bottom lip in an attempt to stem the tears. Over this we hear* SHIRLEY.

SHIRLEY (*VO*)   God, can't you be evil when you're a kid? I used to pick on Marjorie somethin' rotten.

As she continues speaking . . .

27 *Interior classroom, school – day*

It is the end of term. The PUPILS, *including* YOUNG SHIRLEY, *are seated at their desks. The* HEADMISTRESS *is standing in front of the class. Also in front of them stands* MARJORIE. *The* HEADMISTRESS *is holding* MARJORIE'S *end of term report. Over this, we hear* SHIRLEY.

SHIRLEY (*VO*)   And all the time, I suppose I really wanted to be *like* her.

HEADMISTRESS   Your report is excellent – as usual. And I am particularly delighted to learn that you are going to stay on with us to take 'A' levels – which will lead to your eventual entry into university. Congratulations, my dear.

MARJORIE (*with a nice smile*)   Thank you, Miss.

She takes her report, returns to her desk and sits down beside SHIRLEY.

HEADMISTRESS   And now we come to Miss Valentine.

As YOUNG SHIRLEY *gets up and comes forward, the* HEADMISTRESS *glances at the report.*

HEADMISTRESS   Well, Shirley – naturally you *are* leaving us. And a brief glance at your report confirms my deep suspicion that you will not go far in life.

YOUNG SHIRLEY *shrugs.*

HEADMISTRESS   And perhaps it's just as well, for, given your marks in Geography, you'll truly get lost.

She holds out the report, smirking at her own joke. SHIRLEY *snatches the report.*

YOUNG SHIRLEY   Well, tickle my tits till Friday!

She walks to the back of the class and then heads for the door. The girls titter.

HEADMISTRESS   Miss Valentine – will you please come back?

28 *Interior school corridor – day*

YOUNG SHIRLEY *enters the corridor – stops. Tears her report into pieces then walks away throwing the bits into the air.*

End of flashback

29 *Interior SHIRLEY'S kitchen – day*

SHIRLEY *walks to open hall door, switches on the kitchen light then walks back.*

SHIRLEY   'Course, after I left I never saw any more of her – Marjorie Majors. Then, a few weeks ago, I was on me way home from the town – you know loaded down with shopping.

As she is speaking . . .

Flashback

30 *Exterior Adelphi Hotel – day*

It is pouring with rain. SHIRLEY *comes along, weighed down with two loaded carrier bags of shopping. She is wearing a mac, her hair is soaking wet, bedraggled, hanging in limp strands, the rain running down her face. She walks to the edge of the pavement and raises her arm.*

SHIRLEY   Ta – taxi – taxi.

Taxi drives right past leaving SHIRLEY *on the pavement in front of the hotel, dripping.*
   A big chauffeur-driven limousine drives past . . . The wheels hit a

puddle and the water sprays over SHIRLEY. SHIRLEY *stamps her feet and looks at the limo.*

SHIRLEY   Oh, sod it!

The car stops at the entrance of the hotel. A uniformed DOORMAN *hurries forward with an open umbrella, opens the passenger door.* SHIRLEY *stands watching as from the car steps a vision of elegance, beautifully dressed, groomed, coiffured. It is* MARJORIE MAJORS. *Sheltered by the* DOORMAN'S *umbrella, she turns to* SHIRLEY.

MARJORIE   I'm terribly sorry.

We see SHIRLEY'S *face. She is dumbfounded.* MARJORIE, *under the umbrella, steps forward and she and* SHIRLEY *come face to face. For a long moment they stand staring at each other.*

MARJORIE   Forgive me for asking, but didn't you used to be Shirley Valentine?
SHIRLEY   Marjorie Majors! I'd recognise those elocution lessons anywhere.

MARJORIE *laughs, her face warm and smiling.*

MARJORIE   It is! It's Shirley! My God, you're drenched! Come in and have tea.

MARJORIE *takes* SHIRLEY'S *arm and leads her into the hotel.*

31   *Interior elevator, Adelphi Hotel – day*

There are four people in the elevator as it ascends: the elegant MARJORIE, *the wet, bedraggled* SHIRLEY, *and a formally dressed* BUSINESS MAN *in his forties and his wife. A puddle of water forms at* SHIRLEY'S *feet. They eye it and* SHIRLEY *with disapproval. The* BUSINESS MAN *eyes* MARJORIE *with interest.*

SHIRLEY   (*VO*)   Well, Marjorie, you've waited a long time for your revenge, but you've got me in good style now. Oh, go on dig the knife in quick and let's get it over with. Tell me all about you – bein' an air hostess on Concorde.

29

But MARJORIE *is looking at* SHIRLEY *with a warm, friendly smile.*

MARJORIE   I can't believe it! Shirley! After all these years.

SHIRLEY   I know – an' I haven't changed a bit have I? Still kept my youthful complexion.

MARJORIE   We've got to get you out of those wet things – Here we are.

The elevator stops and the doors open. The BUSINESS MAN *stands aside, smiling admiringly at* MARJORIE. *She gives him a nice smile and steps out.* SHIRLEY *follows.*

32 *Interior sitting room of* MARJORIE'S *suite, Adelphi Hotel – day*

MARJORIE *is curled up at one end of a big settee. She takes foil off a bottle of champagne and puts it in an ice bucket. A waitress pushes a low trolley with a tray of afternoon tea.* SHIRLEY *comes out of the bathroom. She is wearing a luxurious red towelling robe and her hair is wrapped in a towel.*

SHIRLEY   Thanks Marjorie.

MARJORIE *stands and looks at* SHIRLEY.

MARJORIE *(looking at Shirley)*   Well, that's better.

SHIRLEY *looks at the waitress and waves.*

SHIRLEY *(to* WAITRESS*)*   Hello.

WAITRESS *bends over the tea trolley setting it up.*

MARJORIE   Now I want to know everything that's happened to you. I want the whole story from A to Z.

SHIRLEY   Got a postage stamp? I'll write it down for you.

MARJORIE   Won't you sit down Shirley?

SHIRLEY *sits on the settee and* MARJORIE *sits down besides her.*

MARJORIE   Do you have children?

SHIRLEY   Yeah.

30

MARJORIE   Tell me about them. Are they like you?

SHIRLEY   Oh well, our Millandra's a bit of a mare – and Brian's a headcase. So, yeah, they *are* like me.

MARJORIE *laughs.*

MARJORIE   Well, this is great isn't it?

SHIRLEY   Yeah.

SHIRLEY   So, . . . so where, where, . . . Where are you off to next?

MARJORIE   Paris, tonight I'm afraid.

SHIRLEY   Is that where you live now?

MARJORIE   No, I'm based in London. But eh . . . I travel all over. From Paris it's Athens, I think.

SHIRLEY (*unsure*)   That's Greece, isn't it?

MARJORIE   Yes.

SHIRLEY (*smiling*)   I remember from Geography. All those islands.

MARJORIE (*smiling, too*)   That's right.

WAITRESS *at tea trolley addresses* MARJORIE.

WAITRESS   Shall I pour now Madam?

MARJORIE   Please.

SHIRLEY *looks at the* WAITRESS *and points to* MARJORIE.

SHIRLEY   This is my friend Marjorie. We were at school together. Now she's an air hostess on Concorde.

MARJORIE   Pardon darling? An air hostess? My God Shirley, whatever gave you that idea? I certainly travel widely, but I'm not an air hostess. Darling, I'm a hooker . . . I'm a whore.

She smiles and we see the shocked waitress pour the tea into the sandwiches.

WAITRESS   Oh Madam, I'm . . . I'm . . . I'm so sorry . . . I'll get you some more.

MARJORIE   Never mind, just leave it. What do we want tea for anyway? This calls for a celebration.

31

MARJORIE *goes to the bottle of champagne in the ice bucket – picks it up, uncorks it and starts to pour out the champagne.*

SHIRLEY (*with bewildered admiration*)   I just can't believe it. You. A hooker. Honest, Marjorie?
MARJORIE (*laughing*)   Yes – honest.
SHIRLEY   And all that money your mother spent on elocution lessons!

They both laugh as MARJORIE *brings the drinks across, gives one to* SHIRLEY *and curls up on the settee again.*

MARJORIE   D'you know something? I always hated the way I had to speak. I still do.
SHIRLEY   I think you speak lovely. (*she smiles*) You – Marjorie Majors – a whore.
MARJORIE (*laughing*)   A top class hooker, of course. Mind you I always *was* top of the class, wasn't I?

They clink glasses and drink.

MARJORIE   Are you shocked darling?
SHIRLEY   No. No. I'm not. I was just thinking about all those house points.

SHIRLEY *leans forward, nudges* MARJORIE *with her elbow and they both laugh.*

Dissolve to:
towel on chair. SHIRLEY *is sitting on the settee drinking champagne, but is wearing a frock.*

MARJORIE   Found it!

MARJORIE *comes out of the bedroom with a photo album. She sits beside* SHIRLEY *and they look at it.*

SHIRLEY   Is that *our* class?
MARJORIE   Yes.
SHIRLEY   Oh my God.

We see the photograph of schoolgirls with teachers in the front row and the headmistress.

SHIRLEY (*off*)   Look at my hair!
MARJORIE (*off*)   There's your favourite.
SHIRLEY   Yeah, the cow, Miss Dearden.

MARJORIE *smokes as she sits beside* SHIRLEY.

SHIRLEY   Remember Marjorie? Smoking is bad for your health.
MARJORIE   God – what a pain in the neck I was.
SHIRLEY   No you weren't. You know I never forgave myself for what I did to that beautiful soufflé of yours.

Telephone rings off. MARJORIE *starts to rise. She walks over and lifts the receiver.*

MARJORIE (*into phone*)   Yes? Yes . . . Oh right. Tell him I'll be down in five minutes. (*she replaces the receiver*) Hell, it's my car for the airport.

MARJORIE *sits again beside* SHIRLEY.

MARJORIE   Oh I wish I didn't have to go. It's been such a lovely afternoon.
SHIRLEY   Yeah, and do you know, when I first saw you, I almost fled.
MARJORIE   Why?
SHIRLEY   Oh, I don't know. I thought you'd come – lording it over me.
MARJORIE   Me lording it over you. Don't you realise I always wanted to be like you.
SHIRLEY   And I wanted to be like *you*. If only we'd known, we could've been great mates – you know, real close.
MARJORIE   It's been fun hasn't it.
SHIRLEY   Yeah. Hey you're off to Paris now. That's lovely.
MARJORIE   Yes, but I'd rather be *here* – talking to you.
SHIRLEY   Well then.

33 *Exterior Adelphi Hotel – day*

It is not raining now, though the road is still wet. MARJORIE'S *limousine is at the entrance. A* HOTEL PORTER *is holding the door open for* MARJORIE. *They stop by the car.*

MARJORIE Can we give you a lift?

SHIRLEY No. I'm fine thanks. I've still got a bit of shopping to do.

MARJORIE Well then.

MARJORIE *turns to* SHIRLEY, *puts her hands on* SHIRLEY'S *arms and kisses her on the cheek. We hear:*

SHIRLEY *(VO)* And there was real affection in that kiss. It was the sweetest kiss I'd known in years.

MARJORIE *holds* SHIRLEY *away and looks at her with a little smile.*

MARJORIE Goodbye, Shirley . . . Goodbye, Shirley Valentine.

A moment, then she turns and gets into the car. The DOORMAN *shuts the door, salutes and steps back. The car moves away.*

SHIRLEY *(VO)* Goodbye, Shirley Valentine . . .

In a CLOSE SHOT *we see* SHIRLEY *watching the car go. Her eyes fill with tears.*

SHIRLEY *(VO)* What happened to her? What's happened to Shirley Valentine? She got married – to a boy called Joe.

34 *Interior bus, city centre – day*

The bus is fairly full. SHIRLEY *is sitting by herself, her shopping bags on the seat beside her. Her cheeks are still tear-stained. She is looking out of the window.*

From her point of view we see that it is raining again, the water streaming down the window. The bus is travelling along a busy, well-lit city street.

SHIRLEY *is gazing at her reflection in the window, her thoughts far away. We hear:*

SHIRLEY (*VO*) And even though her name was changed to Bradshaw she was still Shirley Valentine. For a while. She knew who she was. But somewhere along the way, the boy called Joe turned into – 'him'. And Shirley Valentine turned into – this . . .

SHIRLEY *stares at her reflection for a long moment.*

35 *Exterior street – night*

SHIRLEY *is carrying her shopping bags.*

SHIRLEY (*VO*) An' what I can't remember is the day or the week or the month or the year when it happened, when it stopped bein' any good.

36 *Exterior shop – night*

As rain starts again SHIRLEY *stands in shop doorway.*

SHIRLEY (*VO*) When Shirley Valentine disappeared – became just another name on the missin' persons list.

SHIRLEY *looks up to* CAMERA.

SHIRLEY (*to* CAMERA) He says he still loves me. You know. He doesn't. It's just somethin' he says. It's funny isn't it, 'I love you'. Like it makes everythin' all right. Like you can be beaten and battered and half insane – and if you complain he'll say, 'What's wrong? You know I love you'.

37 *Exterior shopping street – night*

SHIRLEY *walks on in the rain.*

SHIRLEY I love you! They should bottle it and sell it. It cures everything.

End of flashback

38 *Interior* SHIRLEY'S *kitchen – evening*

A CLOSE SHOT *of* SHIRLEY *as she looks at three eggs frying.*

SHIRLEY   And, I know what you're thinkin'. Why don't I leave him? Well, I'm, terrified if you want to know. I'm terrified that if I left him there would be nowhere for me to go. No place for me in the life beyond the wall. (*she looks down at the frying pan*) When I was a girl, I used to jump off our roof.

We see Joe through frosted glass door.

JOE   Is it ready then?

JOE *opens door and stands in the doorway.*

JOE   I get me tea at six o'clock and it's near ten past. What's goin' on?

SHIRLEY *puts eggs on two plates of chips.*

SHIRLEY   It's ready. Sit down.

As JOE *comes forward and sits at the end of the table,* SHIRLEY *picks up the two plates of chips and egg, puts one with the two eggs in front of* JOE, *the other at the other end of the table for herself and sits down. She starts to put sauce on her meal, but* JOE *just sits staring at his plate.* SHIRLEY *looks at him.*

JOE   What's this, then?
SHIRLEY   What?
JOE   What . . . is . . . this?

SHIRLEY *leans forward and peers at* JOE'S *plate.*

SHIRLEY   Well it looks very like chips an'egg to me – but maybe it's a trick question.
JOE   It's Thursday. We have steak on Thursday. We always have steak on Thursday.
SHIRLEY   Well, all right, it's Thursday. But we're havin' chips an'egg for a change. You *like* chips an'egg.

JOE   On a Tuesday – I like chips an'egg. Today is Thursday.

SHIRLEY   Well, pretend it's Tuesday.

JOE   Where's my steak?

SHIRLEY (*a moment – then . . .*)   I give it to the dog.

JOE   What dog?

SHIRLEY   Gillian's dog across the street.

JOE (*gradually building to eruption*)   Is this it? Have you finally gone round the friggin' pipe? Look at me, I'm workin' from mornin' till night, pullin' out me tripe – and what do I find? You talkin' to the walls! Givin' my tea to any friggin' stray dog that comes along – and I'm expected to eat *this!*

He jabs a finger at his plate.

JOE   Well, I'm *not* eatin' this. I – am – not – eatin' – shite!

With a violent shove, he pushes his plate along the length of the table. It hits SHIRLEY's plate and both plates and their contents tip into SHIRLEY's lap. For a moment she sits still, looking at him. Then, quite calmly, she gets up, a small determined smile on her face. The egg yolks are running down her skirt, some of the chips clinging to the sticky mess. As JOE continues talking, she moves across to the cupboard. JOE sits back in his chair, his hands on the table.

JOE   Chips an' egg. Chips an' friggin' egg . . . When I'm workin' all the hours that God sends.

SHIRLEY *opens the cupboard and with an egg soaked chip underlines the word 'Greece' on the poster.*

JOE   I don't know why I bother. I don't know what I'm doin' any of it for.

He suddenly notices what SHIRLEY is doing.

JOE   What's that?

SHIRLEY *steps back, speaking calmly, but with steel in her voice.*

SHIRLEY   It's a place . . . It's a place I'm goin' to.

JOE (*building up gradually*) Oh, I get it. That's the name of the game, is it? I'm not gettin' fed properly, 'cos *you're* savin' for a foreign friggin' holiday.

He gets to his feet.

JOE Well, I'm tellin' you now, you can forget it. (*shouting, emphasising each word and pointing at the poster*) I am not goin' to no Greece!

He stamps across the room and stands by the open door.

JOE Get it.

He goes out slamming the door behind him.

39 Exterior street, city centre – day

SHIRLEY *walks along and enters a store. She picks up a wire basket, then goes in.*

40 Interior chemist's shop – day

SHIRLEY *is selecting a bottle of suntan oil from among the creams and lotions displayed on a stand.*

41 Interior bookshop – day

Open on a CLOSE SHOT *of the shelves devoted to travel books:* SHIRLEY'S *hand comes in reaching for a Greek phrase book.* CAMERA *pulls back to bring her in as she takes the book from the shelf and opens it, mouths a few words then closes it.*

42 Exterior Passport Office – day

SHIRLEY *comes out holding and looking at her passport.*

43 Exterior department store – day

SHIRLEY *is browsing in the ladies' underwear department. She moves to the shelves of panties and picks out a pair. She holds them up. We see that they are very attractive, lace-edged. As she considers them,* GILLIAN'S *voice comes from behind her.*

GILLIAN (*off*)   Oh, hello, Shirley . . .

SHIRLEY *swings round to* GILLIAN.

GILLIAN   What are you doin' here?
SHIRLEY (*off her guard*)   I . . . I . . . I. I'm just buying a few things.

She goes to put the panties back on the shelf, but GILLIAN *puts her hand out and holds them.*

GILLIAN   Oh, they're quite nice, aren't they? It's marvellous what they can do with man-made fibres these days, isn't it? (*she feels the material*) You'd almost think it was silk – if you weren't familiar with the real thing.

She releases her hold. SHIRLEY'S *eyes are cold.*

GILLIAN   Well I expect they're quite nice for your Millandra.
SHIRLEY   Oh no, Gillian, I'm not buying them for Millandra. I'm buying them for myself.

Gillian takes a pointed look at SHIRLEY'S *figure.* SHIRLEY *tosses the panties back on the shelf and picks up a very brief, really sexy pair of black lace panties. She holds them up.*

SHIRLEY   Oh these are better.

GILLIAN   Yes?
SHIRLEY (*to* GILLIAN *with a casual smile*)   Yes, but I shan't be *wearing* them for myself. I shall be wearing them for . . . for my lover.

GILLIAN'S *jaw drops, her eyes wide with astonishment.*

SHIRLEY   Yes, we fly out tomorrow – my lover and I. For a fortnight on the Greek Islands. Just two weeks of sun, sand and taramasalata – and whatever else takes our fancy.

She picks up her basket, tosses the panties into it. GILLIAN *stands, struck dumb.*

SHIRLEY   Oh well, I must be off now Gillian, still got a few more things to buy. I don't suppose you noticed which counter the suspender belts are on did you?

GILLIAN, *speechless, shakes her head.*

SHIRLEY   No? Oh, well, I'm sure I'll find them. Ta ra Gillian.

She makes a perfect exit. Behind her, GILLIAN *stands staring after her in astonishment.*

44 *Interior* SHIRLEY'S *hall and stairs – day*

SHIRLEY *struggles down the stairs with a heavy suitcase and a bulging travel bag and a hat. She dumps the suitcase in the hall and goes through to the kitchen.*

45 *Interior* SHIRLEY'S *kitchen – day*

SHIRLEY *enters puts her travel bag and hat on the table and her handbag in front of her. She is inwardly excited. She takes a bundle of packages from her handbag, puts them on the table and checks them over, talking to herself.*

SHIRLEY   Passport . . . tickets . . . money . . . passport . . . tickets . . . money . . .

She looks up and speaks to the CAMERA.

SHIRLEY   Four o'clock Jane's pickin' me up.

She glances at her wrist watch and talks to herself.

SHIRLEY   Ten past eleven.

She clutches her stomach.

SHIRLEY   Oh, I feel sick.

She walks to the sink and starts wiping down the surfaces.

SHIRLEY Those travel pills mustn't be workin'. I still feel sick and I've taken four already and I've only travelled up and down the stairs.

She starts checking again as she wipes the table.

SHIRLEY Passport . . . tickets . . . money.
Got a full one, Wall – Proper passport –

She moves over to the refrigerator and wipes it down.

SHIRLEY Well, you never know, Shirley. This could be the start of something. This year, Greece – next year, the World!

She stops cleaning fridge, suddenly depressed and turns to the CAMERA.

SHIRLEY *(to herself)* Oh God – I know I should've told him.

She opens the freezer and indicates various packs, each clearly labelled.

SHIRLEY Ten days I've been secretly ironing and packin'! It's been like livin' in bleedin' prison. Look, cooking all his meals for the next fortnight. They're all in the freezer. Me mother's goin' to defrost them and do his cookin' for him.

She closes the fridge.

SHIRLEY With a bit o'luck he won't even notice I'm not here.

She walks to the sink area and starts cleaning around.

SHIRLEY Oh God . . . God look I know I'm bein' cruel and I'll have to pay for it when I get back. I don't mind payin' for it then but just . . . just do me a favour, God, an' don't make me have to pay for it durin' the two weeks. Keep everyone safe, please.

The front door bell rings loudly. For a moment SHIRLEY *stands paralysed. She gathers up her papers into her handbag then picks up her hat and travel bag.*

46 *Interior SHIRLEY'S hall and stairs – day*

SHIRLEY *hurries out of the kitchen, grabs up her suitcase and travel bag and pushes them into the cupboard under the stairs. She puts on an overall over her travel suit. The front door bell rings again.* SHIRLEY *goes to the front door, takes a deep breath and opens it.* MILLANDRA *is standing outside, at her feet a pile of luggage – a battered suitcase, a duffle bag, a couple of plastic carrier bags. Hanging round her neck is a small personal cassette player, with the earphones also around her neck.* SHIRLEY *stares at her blankly.*

MILLANDRA   I hate that Sharon Louise. She's a mare. I don't know why I ever went to live with her in the first place.

Suddenly she puts her arms round SHIRLEY.

MILLANDRA   Mother – I've come back to live with *you.*

She buries her face in SHIRLEY'S *shoulder with a dramatic sob.* SHIRLEY *pats* MILLANDRA'S *back.*

MILLANDRA   Mother – will ya make me some cocoa an' toast – like you used to?

She moves past SHIRLEY.

MILLANDRA   I'm goin' to me room.

She runs up the stairs. SHIRLEY *turns and looks at the luggage outside the front door. With a sigh, she picks up the suitcase and brings it into the hall.*

47 *Interior MILLANDRA'S bedroom – day*

MILLANDRA *is in bed, propped up on four pillows. She is reading an old Annual. Her clothes – jeans, shirt, sweater – are strewn about the floor.* SHIRLEY *carries in a mug of cocoa.* MILLANDRA *takes the cocoa.* SHIRLEY *moves over to the window, gloomily looking out to the street.* MILLANDRA looks across at SHIRLEY.

MILLANDRA   She's a cow, that Sharon Louise. I don't know why I ever left you, mother.

She sips the cocoa. She makes a face.

MILLANDRA Mother, you haven't put enough sugar in this cocoa. Will you go down and get us another spoon?

She holds her mug out to SHIRLEY, *going back to reading her magazine as she does so.* SHIRLEY *crosses, takes the mug and moves to the door.*

48 *Interior* SHIRLEY'S *kitchen – day*

SHIRLEY *is at the table, putting another spoonful of sugar into the mug of cocoa. She looks across at the* WALL.

SHIRLEY What am I doin' Wall? She's only been back two minutes and she's got me struttin' round like R-two bleedin' D-two.

She picks up the mug of cocoa and moves to the door.

49 *Interior* MILLANDRA'S *bedroom – day*

MILLANDRA *is propped up in bed.* SHIRLEY *enters with the cocoa. She takes the mug of cocoa from* SHIRLEY. MILLANDRA *sips her cocoa.* SHIRLEY *moves over to the window and looks out.*

MILLANDRA Oh thanks, mother, that's brilliant. Oh I love bein' back home. We'll go down town on Saturday, shall we, mother – like we used to? Do some shoppin' together, eh? Just you an' me.

SHIRLEY Yes. That'll be . . .

MILLANDRA Mother, do us a favour and bring the telly upstairs for us, will you?

SHIRLEY *sits on a chair at the end of the bed.*

SHIRLEY Millandra . . . Millandra, I'm really pleased you've come back home, because – I've missed you.

MILLANDRA Oh I've missed *you*, Mother. I've been homesick, you know.

SHIRLEY I . . . I mean, I've never said that. I've, I've never complained, because I believe that kids should have their own lives. (*Millandra looks at her watch*) But there's been many's the time that I'd have loved to have sat and had a talk with you or, or gone to town with you or had a meal with you or shared a laugh . . .

MILLANDRA *is looking at her wristwatch.*

MILLANDRA Mother . . .

SHIRLEY Just like, like – not as your mother, but as another human bein'.

MILLANDRA Oh Mother, could you get the telly for us? Playschool's gonna be on in a minute.

SHIRLEY (*following her own theme*) But I couldn't because you had your own life. Your own interests – and your own friends – none of it to do with *me*.

MILLANDRA Yeh, well, that's okay, 'cos now I've come back home.

SHIRLEY Yes, you've come home! And that's fantastic. And . . . and . . . you couldn't have picked a better time for it. It'll . . . It'll be a great help havin' you here to look after your father.

MILLANDRA Why? What's wrong with him?

SHIRLEY Oh, there's nothin' wrong with him. It's . . . it's just with me not bein' here for the next two weeks.

MILLANDRA, *suddenly interested, stares at* SHIRLEY.

MILLANDRA What?

SHIRLEY *gets up from the bed.*

SHIRLEY With me and Jane goin' to Greece today . . .

MILLANDRA You and . . . ? Goin' to Greece? What for?

SHIRLEY (*with a beaming smile*) For two . . . whole . . . weeks!

MILLANDRA That Jane – and you? And what's me father had to say about it?

SHIRLEY (*still smiling*)   Well I haven't told him.

For a moment MILLANDRA *stares at her, then she throws the bedclothes aside, jumps out and grabs up her jeans.*

MILLANDRA   I think it's a disgrace!
SHIRLEY   What?
MILLANDRA   My own mother, behavin' like that!
SHIRLEY   Millandra, I thought you'd be made up for me.
MILLANDRA   Made up? Made up? I think it's disgustin'!

She grabs her shoes and puts them on.

SHIRLEY   Hold on – what's disgustin' about it?

MILLANDRA *puts her sweater on.*

MILLANDRA   Two middle-aged women goin' to Greece on their own. It's disgustin'!
SHIRLEY   Oh, don't be silly, love. Where are you going?

MILLANDRA *picks up another sweater and her jacket.*

MILLANDRA   I'm going back to my flat.

She crosses to the door.

50 *Interior* SHIRLEY'S *stairs and hall – day*

MILLANDRA, *carrying her sweater, comes to the top of the stairs.*

MILLANDRA   Greece! At *your* age! You an' that Jane! It's obscene!

As she starts down the stairs, SHIRLEY *appears at the head of them. Angry now, she shouts down at* MILLANDRA.

SHIRLEY   You are jumpin' to exactly the same conclusions your father would. You think I'm goin' to Greece on a 'grab a granny fortnight'!

MILLANDRA *carries her bags to the front door and throws them out.*

51 *Exterior SHIRLEY'S house and street – day*

SHIRLEY'S *bedroom window is opened and* SHIRLEY *leans out and shouts after her daughter.*

SHIRLEY   That's right, Millandra . . .! I'm goin' to Greece for the sex!

In a quick cut we see a VAN DRIVER *is delivering a box to a house along the street.* MILLANDRA *passes the rear of the van and stops to look up at* SHIRLEY.
SHIRLEY *shouts after the retreating* MILLANDRA.

SHIRLEY   Sex for breakfast, sex for lunch, sex for dinner and sex for supper!

The VAN DRIVER *shouts up at* SHIRLEY, *grinning.*

VAN DRIVER   Sounds like a marvellous diet, love!

SHIRLEY, *suddenly smiling broadly, shouts down to him.*

SHIRLEY   It is! Have you never heard of it? It's called the F Plan!

She starts to close the window.

52 *Interior SHIRLEY'S bedroom – day*

SHIRLEY *pulls her head in and shuts the window. She turns away to cross the room. She props herself on her elbows on the bed. She looks at herself in her mirror. Looking suddenly unsure of herself, she talks to her reflection in the mirror.*

SHIRLEY   You? Goin' to Greece? What for? What the hell am I goin' for? Shirley, you are one silly bitch. You're forty-two not twenty-two. You're just another stupid woman looking for adventure. And the time for adventure is over. Well I'll phone Jane tell her I'm not coming.

She gets off bed and exits.

53 *Interior* SHIRLEY'S *kitchen – day*

SHIRLEY *picks up the receiver and starts to dial. The front door bell rings. She puts the receiver down. Then, after a moment, she gets to her feet and crosses without interest to the door.*

54 *Interior* SHIRLEY'S *hall and sitting room – day*

SHIRLEY *comes along the hall to the front door and opens it.* GILLIAN *is standing on the doorstep, one hand behind her back.* SHIRLEY *looks at her coldly.*

GILLIAN   Oh, hello, Shirley. Is Joe at home?
SHIRLEY (*with an ironic smile*)   No, Gillian – Joe isn't at home . . .

GILLIAN *moves past* SHIRLEY *into the hall and closes the front door behind her, they walk towards the sitting room.*

SHIRLEY   . . . and listen if you've come to spill the beans, don't bother . . .
GILLIAN (*interrupting*)   Shirley, I haven't come to spill any beans. I just wanted to check that Joseph wasn't home – before I gave you *this*.

In the sitting room from behind her back GILLIAN *produces a flat dress box.* SHIRLEY *looks at it, puzzled, then at* GILLIAN *questioningly.* SHIRLEY *takes the box, looks at* GILLIAN *not understanding.*

GILLIAN   I want you to have it. For your trip – to Greece. Well do open it.

SHIRLEY *puts the box on a coffee table and removes the lid. Inside is a silk robe. Gingerly,* SHIRLEY *lifts it out and holds it up. It is beautiful and obviously an expensive garment.*

GILLIAN   It is silk. It's never been worn. You see – I was never brave enough.
SHIRLEY (*overcome*)   Oh, Gillian . . .
GILLIAN   I wish . . . I wish I'd had *your* bravery.
SHIRLEY (*about to confess*)   Listen . . . I've . . .

GILLIAN *cuts in.*

GILLIAN Please Shirley don't say anything. It's yours. I just wanted you to know that − I think you're marvellous.

They walk into the hall and towards the door.

SHIRLEY Gillian!

GILLIAN *goes, shutting the door behind her. For a moment,* SHIRLEY *doesn't move, just stands, caressing the robe, feeling its texture. Then, slowly, she returns to the hall mirror and puts on the robe, looking at herself in the mirror. Her eyes light up. She smiles with growing confidence and delight. We hear:*

SHIRLEY (*VO*) Gillian really believes it! All that rubbish about me takin' a lover! She really believes it's possible! In her eyes I'm no longer Shirley Bradshaw − middle-aged housewife, beginnin' to sag a bit − I'm Shirley the Brave, Shirley the Marvellous! . . . Shirley Valentine! From now on, when I look in the mirror, I'm not goin' to say 'Christ, you're forty-two' − I'm goin' to say, 'Hey Shirley, you're only forty-two! (*she takes off the robe*) Isn't that marvellous?'

55 *Interior* SHIRLEY'S **kitchen − day**

SHIRLEY *sticks a white gum label on the poster of Greece inside her cupboard. We see the message which reads 'Gone to Greece. Back in two weeks'.* SHIRLEY *picks up the clothes from the table. Smiles then exits.*

56 *Exterior* SHIRLEY'S **house − evening**

JOE *gets out of his car in the pouring rain, runs across the road and opens his front door.*

57 *Interior* SHIRLEY'S **hall and kitchen − evening**

JOE *closes front door, switches on hall lights and throws his keys on the table, then walks towards the kitchen.*

JOE   Shirl.

He puts his briefcase down.

JOE   Shirl.

He switches on kitchen light and walks into the kitchen. He stops and looks at the note then tears it off the poster and crumples it up. He walks over to the window and we see his face reflected in the rain-swept glass.

58 *Exterior* GREECE: *beach and cove – day*

We see the shimmer of the midday sun on a calm sea. The CAMERA *tracks back to reveal people swimming and playing in the sea. People on the beach. A man sitting under a beach umbrella, a woman lying under an umbrella. Rocks and sand.*

SHIRLEY (*off*) Hello . . .

We close in on SHIRLEY *sitting on a chair under a sun umbrella in dark glasses. She speaks to the* CAMERA.

SHIRLEY Bet you didn't recognise me.

She takes off her sunglasses.

SHIRLEY I hardly recognise *meself* these days . . . I love it here.

She turns and speaks in turn to the ROCK *beside her and to the* CAMERA.

SHIRLEY Don't I, Rock?

She indicates the rock and speaks to the CAMERA.

SHIRLEY That's Rock. We met the first day I got here. I found this little place – (*to the* ROCK) I found *you*, didn't I, Rock? I talk to you . . . Rock. (*to the* CAMERA) He's got his name running right through him. Now of course, *I* talk to *Rock*, but he doesn't talk to *me*. He can't, you see. He's a Greek rock – He can't understand a bleedin' word I'm sayin'. I might have risked the main beach if I'd been with Jane. But on me own I felt a bit – you know – conspicuous . . . Well 'cause Jane

met a feller, didn't she? Not here. On the plane. Honest to
God.

Flashback

59 *Interior aircraft in flight – day*

The aircraft is full of PASSENGERS *going on holiday. Two or three* AIR
HOSTESSES *are in attendance. An executive type followed by Jane walks
up the aisle – he sits down.* JANE *continues up the aisle and sits beside*
SHIRLEY. *She looks very pleased with herself.* SHIRLEY *turns to her.*

SHIRLEY   Where've you been?
JANE   I told you. Just to the loo.
SHIRLEY   I was beginnin' to think you'd fallen down it.

As she speaks, we see the EXECUTIVE *type at his seat smiling.* JANE
indicates him to SHIRLEY.

JANE (*quietly*)   Shirley . . . Shirley – you see *him*?
SHIRLEY   What, the walking groin?
JANE   Shirl! Listen – he's just invited me out to dinner.
SHIRLEY (*taken aback*)   What!
JANE   Tonight. He's got a villa – on the other side of the island
from us – with an olive grove.

SHIRLEY *looks unbelievingly at* CAMERA.

JANE   Well Shirl, it's only for tonight. We'll still do all the
things we planned. You don't mind do you?

Already, SHIRLEY *is seething with suppressed anger.*

SHIRLEY   Listen, Jane – I think you've probably blown the
Feminist of The Year Award, so just leave it out, will you. I
mean, obviously, it's been difficult time for you since your
feller ran off with the milkman . . .

The PASSENGERS *sitting near them are entranced.* THELMA *who is sat
behind* SHIRLEY *and* JANE *reacts with interest to this revelation.*

SHIRLEY . . . and now you've got this opportunity, I don't want you to give another thought to *me*. You go to his villa and enjoy yourself. Give his olives a good pressin'!

JANE (*happily*) Shirley – thanks for being so understanding.

SHIRLEY *looks at her with blank astonishment.*

60 *Interior Athens Airport, baggage reclaim area – day*

PASSENGERS *are collecting their bags from the counter, loading them on to trolleys or carrying them away. Among them, we pick up* SHIRLEY. *She has her bag over her shoulder and has her travel bag at her feet. Now she grabs her suitcase from the counter. She starts to follow other* PASSENGERS. JANE *hurries forward after her.*

JANE Shirley . . . Shirley, where are you going? We said we'd give you a lift to the ferry.

SHIRLEY (*on her dignity*) No. I'm fine on me own – thanks.

She struggles determinedly away. JANE *exits to see about her own luggage.*

61 *Exterior ferry – day*

SHIRLEY *stands at the bow of the ferry as it approaches Mykonos. The other* PASSENGERS *including* DOUGIE *and* JEANETTE, SYDNEY *and* THELMA *and their children mill about.* SHIRLEY *pays no attention to anyone as she stares at the approaching island, her face a mask of sheer delight.*

62 *Exterior Mykonos – day*

We see the bay of Mykonos, then we see a coach travelling along the coastal road.

63 *Interior coach – day*

SHIRLEY *is standing looking out at the passing scene with delight. In the front seats beside her are two holidaymakers –* DOUGIE *and* JEANETTE. *After a moment,* DOUGIE *half rises and taps* SHIRLEY *on the shoulder.*

DOUGIE   Here y'are, love. You sit here.
SHIRLEY   Oh, no, no, thanks. I'd rather stand. I can see more.

With a shrug, DOUGIE *sits down again.* JEANETTE *leans forward and speaks to* SHIRLEY *conspiratorially but loudly.*

JEANETTE   I don't blame you, love. You don't know what's been on these seats, do you? D'you know what I mean?

64 *Exterior coast road – day*

The coach is winding its way along the coast.

65 *Exterior hotel – day*

The coach is pulling up to the hotel. The passengers begin to disembark. SHIRLEY *is followed by* DOUGIE *and* JEANETTE, *who are followed by* SYDNEY, THELMA *and their* CHILDREN.

DOUGIE   We usually go to Lloret. Don't we?
JEANETTE   We couldn't get booked, could we?
SYDNEY   Well, we usually go to Majorca.
THELMA   Oh, aye.
SYDNEY   Right.

SYDNEY, THELMA *and their* TWO KIDS *move and stand in line with* DOUGIE *and* JEANETTE, *surveying the hotel with disapproval.* SHIRLEY *stands apart and looks out across the bay.*

DOUGIE   (*to anyone who will listen*)   Travel agent said we'd like it here. I'm a bit dubious meself.
SYDNEY   (*to all*)   Where's the disco? Where's the bar?
DOUGIE   There's more life in a crematorium.
THELMA   Oh . . . Sydney.
SHIRLEY   (*VO*) (*looking out at the stunning natural beauty of the place, the small harbour below the hotels*)   It was like I'd come to the far side of Paradise. An' I loved it.

End of flashback

66 *Exterior cove – day*

SHIRLEY *is sitting in the cove. She turns and looks at the* CAMERA.

SHIRLEY   Jane never did come back last night, you know – or the next morning. At first I was a bit scared bein' on me own. But then I found this little place.

67 *Exterior quayside – day*

We see SHIRLEY *walking along the quay, crowded with people.*

SHIRLEY *(VO)*   I thought why am I so terrified of being on me own? I'm an expert at it. And then I started to relax.

68 *Exterior cove – day*

SHIRLEY *(to* CAMERA *and* ROCK)   She still hasn't come back, you know. Has she Rock?

She grins.

SHIRLEY   They must be marvellous olives!

69 *Interior hotel dining room – day (evening)*

The room is full of HOLIDAY GUESTS. *As* SHIRLEY *enters, the babble of conversation and laughter suddenly ceases whilst* SHIRLEY, *happily unaware of the other guests staring at her or indicating her, makes her way serenely to her table on the terrace.* RENOS, *the head waiter, follows her.*

SHIRLEY *(VO)*   Funny isn't it? But if you're a woman on your own it doesn't half seem to upset people.

70 *Exterior terrace – evening*

We follow SHIRLEY *until she reaches her table where she turns to* RENOS.

SHIRLEY   Hiya Renos.

Throughout the following, RENOS *places wine onto* SHIRLEY'S *table and then pours a glass of wine for her.*

RENOS (*smiling*)   Good evening, madame. And how are you this evening?

SHIRLEY (*happily*)   Marvellous, thanks. How are you?

RENOS   Good. I am good. I feel a leetle pain in the back, but I say to myself – if I feel a leetle pain in the back, at least it means I am not dead!

They laugh together.

RENOS   Now, madame – tonight I have for you some calamaris. Cooked with a leetle garlic – yes – and butter and lemon. Plenty of lemon. It is beautiful!

SHIRLEY   Lovely.

RENOS *bows to her.*

RENOS   Bon appetit, madame.

SHIRLEY   Thank you.

RENOS *goes out.* SHIRLEY *sips her wine and sits gazing out of the window, taking in the stunning view – completely at peace. The moment is shattered by* JEANETTE'S *voice off screen.*

JEANETTE   Now listen, love, you can't go on like this.

Startled, SHIRLEY *turns and finds* JEANETTE *approaching her. She stops and looks down at* SHIRLEY.

SHIRLEY   Pardon?

JEANETTE   It's not right. We can't help noticing that you are on you're own.

SHIRLEY (*puzzled*)   Who?

JEANETTE   So we've arranged for another chair at our table.

SHIRLEY   Oh no, no thanks very much – I'm . . . .

JEANETTE   We want you to come and join us.

SHIRLEY   No, no thanks very much. I'd really . . . ..

JEANETTE   Now come on, love.

She picks up SHIRLEY'S *glass of wine.*

JEANETTE   I'll take your drink.

She stands waiting as SHIRLEY *reluctantly gets to her feet.* SHIRLEY *walks out.*

71 *Interior hotel dining room – evening*

JEANETTE *starts moving across the room to her table.* SHIRLEY *follows her. As she goes, the* GUESTS *smile at her and start happily talking. As she crosses the room, we hear* SHIRLEY.

SHIRLEY (*VO*)   I wouldn't be surprised if they all burst out into applause – 'cos I've been rescued from me loneliness. Rescued by Dougie and Jeanette from Manchester.

DOUGIE *stands as* SHIRLEY *joins them. They all sit.*

DOUGIE   Make yourself at home. Now have you got a jacuzzi?

SHIRLEY   Er – no . . .

DOUGIE   Well, maybe it's just the thing you've been waiting for. Because *you* always wanted a jacuzzi, didn't you, Jeanette?

JEANETTE   I'd had dreams about gettin' a jacuzzi. Michael Caine's got one, you know.

SHIRLEY   Oh.

DOUGIE   So we get this jacuzzi like . . . but what we found was, we couldn't fit it in our bathroom. So what I did was . . .

JEANETTE   He built an extension!

DOUGIE   I built an extension, didn't I?

SHIRLEY *turns to the* CAMERA.

SHIRLEY   It's a good job we're not havin' soup or I'd put me head in it an' drown meself!

SECOND WAITER *goes to take* JEANETTE'S *uneaten dish.*

SECOND WAITER   Finish?

JEANETTE (*with a grimace of distaste*)   Oh, I couldn't eat *that*.

The SECOND WAITER, *with a small shrug, takes her dish and* DOUGIE'S *and moves away. We see that, at the next table,* SYDNEY *and* THELMA *are listening to* DOUGIE.

DOUGIE You can say what you like – it's not Lloret, is it?

SYDNEY *leans across and speaks loudly to* DOUGIE.

SYDNEY Aye, but the thing is, Dougie, I could like Greece, I could, if it were more like Spain.
DOUGIE I take your point – yeh.
THELMA But it's not, is it?
SYDNEY It's not – an' I'll tell you why. I'll tell you why Greece isn't like Spain. Because Greece well, it's all too Greek. Take me point? An' that's what's wrong with Greece.

SHIRLEY *is listening with growing anger.* SYDNEY *talks even louder.*

SYDNEY It's like them bloody fishin' boats out theer int' bay. I said to *her* this morning . . . (*he gestures at* THELMA) . . . didn't I, Thelma?
THELMA Hmm.
SYDNEY I said to her if you take a close look at side of them boats – you know the bit where it says the name of the boat-builder – I now bet you a pound to a penny it says 'Noah'!

He roars with laughter, joined by THELMA, DOUGIE *and* JEANETTE.

SYDNEY (*to* THELMA) Didn't I say that to you? I bloody did!

SHIRLEY *can stand it no longer. She turns to* SYDNEY, *speaking with emphasis.*

SHIRLEY Excuse me. Excuse me. You do watch the Olympic Games I take it? And you do realise that it was the Greeks who *invented* the Olympic Games?

Now, they are all looking at her.

SHIRLEY Oh, yes Jeanette, they invented a lot of things, the Greeks. Where do you suppose your jacuzzi came from?
JEANETTE M.F.I.

SHIRLEY (*building up now*) But who invented it? The Greeks!
Actually, the Greeks! And it was the Greeks, I'll have you
know – who were responsible for the most important invention of all – the *wheel*!

The others all stare at her, struck dumb. SHIRLEY, *now in top gear,
addresses them all. Around them, the rest of the* GUESTS *are listening now,
fascinated.*

SHIRLEY The English? Don't talk to me about the English?
Because while the Greeks were buildin' roads an' cities an'
temples, what were the English doin'? I'll tell you what the
English were doin'. They were runnin' around in loin-cloths,
ploughin' up the earth with the arse bone of a giraffe!

*She realises how loudly she has been talking. She looks around and sees
that all the* GUESTS *are looking at her. As she subsides in her chair,* RENOS
*appears at her side with three plates of calamaris. He puts a plate of
calamaris in front of her and smiles.*

RENOS Madam.

He puts plates of calamaris in front of DOUGIE *and* JEANETTE. *He goes
to move away but* DOUGIE *raises his hand.*

DOUGIE Hey, mate . . .

RENOS *comes to* DOUGIE'S *side.* DOUGIE *points to his plate.*

DOUGIE What is this?
RENOS Ees calamaris, sir.
DOUGIE I hope not – But what I'm askin' you, Zorba, is – what
is it?

RENOS (*with overdone servility*) Sir – ees calamaris. Ees – er – type
of – feesh.
DOUGIE (*looking at his plate suspiciously*) Well, it don't look much
like fish to me.
RENOS Sir – I can promise you ees fish. This fish was pulled
fresh from sea thees evening by my brother – in a boat called
Noah. (*a brilliant smile*) Enjoy your meal.

JEANETTE, DOUGIE and SHIRLEY *start to eat in silence.*

SHIRLEY *(VO)* For that type you know, if they had been at the last supper they would have asked for chips.

SHIRLEY *picks up her knife and fork and starts to eat. After a moment, so do* DOUGIE *and* JEANETTE, *but with caution.*

SHIRLEY *(with a cheerful smile)* How nice the squid is, isn't it?
JEANETTE Pardon?
SHIRLEY *(pointing at her plate)* I said the squid – the octopus – it's really quite nice.

She puts her hand to her mouth, realising what she has just said. But it is too late. After a moment, JEANETTE *looks down at her plate. Then, with a little moan, she leans back in her chair then slides off it under the table.*

72 *Interior hotel foyer and bar – evening*

From a viewpoint in the foyer we see, in the adjoining bar, a party of around twenty ENGLISH TOURISTS – *among them* DOUGIE *and* JEANETTE, SYDNEY *and* THELMA – *engaged in a high-spirited attempt to dance a traditional Greek dance, to the accompaniment of a small band – piano, violin, accordion, drums. The* TOURISTS *are lined up across the room, arms on each others' shoulders. Among them are two or three of the hotel* WAITERS *trying, with tolerant smiles, to teach the* TOURISTS *the steps.*

SHIRLEY *comes down the stairs into the foyer, carrying a light-weight wool jacket. As she stops and looks through into the bar,* RENOS *comes out. He smiles at her and points towards the dancers.*

RENOS Madame, you will join with your friends?
SHIRLEY *(smiling)* No, I don't think so, Renos. After what I said at dinner-time, I don't think I'd be too popular, do you?
RENOS *(with a chuckle)* Maybe no. *(in Greek, smiling)* Kalinikhti.
SHIRLEY Kalinikhti.

She goes past the dining room, now empty, and onto the terrace.

73 *Exterior SHIRLEY'S hotel and promenade – evening*

SHIRLEY *walks down the road towards the taverna. The road is quite narrow, with a sidewalk between it and the sandy beach. Only an occasional car comes along the road. The sun is low, the taverna is lit and busy.*

74 *Exterior COSTAS'S taverna and sea wall – evening*

There are half a dozen tables on the terrace in front of the taverna.
    SHIRLEY *comes strolling along. Here, the sidewalk is wider and has a low wall with the sea beyond it.* SHIRLEY *pauses, looking down at the sea lapping gently below her. She looks across at the taverna. On a sudden impulse, she crosses to it.*

75 *Interior taverna – evening*

COSTAS, *the owner, sits at a table playing his guitar.*

76 *Exterior taverna – evening*

SHIRLEY *stands outside on the terrace. After a moment* COSTAS, *the owner, comes from the taverna. He comes to her with a polite smile.*

COSTAS   You like something?
SHIRLEY (*smiling, too*)   Er yes – I'd like a drink, please.
COSTAS   Sure eh Gin? Whiskey? What?
SHIRLEY   Erh. No. Wine. Greek, Greek wine.
COSTAS   Ah. Retsina?
SHIRLEY   Will I like that?

SPIRO *appears at the door of the taverna.*

COSTAS (*smiling*)   Is Greek. I think you like.

He turns and nods to SPIRO.

COSTAS   Spiro. Retsina.
SHIRLEY   Eh Eh Eh – excuse me . . .

COSTAS *turns back to her.*

SHIRLEY   I know this sounds a bit soft, but – would you mind – I mean, like would you object if I was to move this table and chair over there by the edge of the sea?

She points down.

COSTAS (*puzzled*)   You want. I move table chair to edge of sea?

SHIRLEY   Yeah.

COSTAS   Why? You don't like my bar?

SHIRLEY   Yes, – it's a lovely bar it is. It's just that I've got this soft little dream about sittin' at a table by the edge of the sea.

COSTAS (*suddenly smiling*)   A dream. So I move table to the edge of the sea – and it make your dream come true?

SHIRLEY   Yeh, I think so.

COSTAS   Sure. Ees no problem.

He nods his head then moves away to speak to SPIRO *in the taverna as* SHIRLEY *exits.*

77 *Exterior sea – sunset*

SHIRLEY *walks to the sea.* SPIRO *enters carrying a table.* COSTAS *follows carrying a chair and wine.* SPIRO *puts the table down by the sea.* COSTAS *puts the chair and wine down.* SPIRO *moves back to taverna.*

SHIRLEY   Thanks.

COSTAS   Oh it ees my pleasure. I move table to sea – and tonight in my bar, I tell the customers – 'Tonight, eh, tonight, I make someone's dream come true.'

COSTAS *gestures to* SHIRLEY *to sit.*

COSTAS   Please.

He waves hand at the sea.

COSTAS   Hmm.

He gives her a little bow and then goes back to the taverna.

SHIRLEY *gathers herself, sits upright, closes her eyes and deeply inhales the sea air. She is willing this moment to be wonderful. Beyond her the sun is low.* SHIRLEY *slowly slumps back into the seat. She glances sideways at the* CAMERA *as if to say, 'All right, so I'm stupid'. She speaks the following not directly to but in the presence of the* CAMERA.

SHIRLEY (*resigned*) Funny isn't it? You know, when you've pictured somethin' – and you've imagined how somethin's gonna be – well, it never turns out like that does it? And for weeks I've pictured myself sitting here – sitting here drinkin' wine by the edge of the sea – An' I knew exactly how it was goin' to feel. I'm here. It doesn't feel a bit like that. I don't feel at all lovely an' serene. I feel pretty daft actually.

We see the setting sun sinking into the clouds at sea level.

SHIRLEY (*VO*) An' awfully old.

78 *Exterior* COSTAS'S *taverna – night*

SHIRLEY *still sits alone at the edge of the sea. She looks up at the moon.*

SHIRLEY (*to herself*) I've lived such a little life. An' even that'll be over pretty soon. I'd allowed myself to live this little life – when inside me there was so much more. An' it's all gone unused. An' now it never will be. Well. Why do we get all this life if we don't ever use it? Why do we all get these . . . feelings and dreams and hopes – if we don't ever use them?

She shakes her head.

SHIRLEY (*to herself*) That's where Shirley Valentine disappeared to. She got lost – in all this unused life.

SHIRLEY *turns to face the sea, fighting back the tears. In respect, the* CAMERA *moves away.*
    The CAMERA *pans and we see* COSTAS *coming out of the taverna. He goes to walk away but stops when he sees* SHIRLEY *still waiting there. He moves across to her and goes to reach for her wine glass. Seeing it is*

still untouched he glances at SHIRLEY. *She is staring fixedly out to sea –
her eyes open wide and her face streaked with tears.* COSTAS *leaves her
glass on the table. He sits a few feet away from* SHIRLEY *and, making
no attempt to talk, stares out to sea with her.*

COSTAS   Dreams they are never in the place you expect them to
be.

*She looks at him. He is smiling. She smiles, too. He stands up and walks
towards her.*

COSTAS   Come I, eh, I escort you to your hotel.
SHIRLEY   Okay.

She stands up. COSTAS *points to himself.*

COSTAS   My name . . . I am Costas Demitriadis.
SHIRLEY *(smiling)*   I'm Shirley . . . hello.
COSTAS   Hello.

They shake hands. He gives her a little bow.
     As they start to stroll along the sidewalk, the CAMERA *pulls back into
a long shot of them.*

79 *Exterior* SHIRLEY'S *hotel and road – night*

*They walk up the road to the hotel. It is quite dark now. The scene is lit
by lights from the hotel.*

SHIRLEY   Thanks for seeing me home.
COSTAS   No I . . . I enjoy.

They arrive at the gate of the hotel where they stop.
COSTAS   So . . . eh tomorrow you want come weez me?
SHIRLEY   Pardon?
COSTAS   I'm – I take brother's boat. We go round island.
SHIRLEY *(a little taken aback)*   Oh no, no thanks. I mean honestly
– you've been really kind. But I couldn't.
COSTAS   Oh is no problem. It's no problem. It's my pleasure.
I um I bring you early . . .

SHIRLEY   No, no, no really . . . I mean I . . . I don't think I should because . . .

She pauses, confused.

COSTAS   You afraid?

SHIRLEY   No, no, no 'course not.

COSTAS (*smiling*)   You afraid – you afraid that I will make foak weez you?

SHIRLEY (*startled*)   What!

COSTAS (*laughs – then . . .*)   Of *course* I want make foak weez you. You are beautiful woman. Oh ay you know. Any man be crazy not to want to make foak weez you.

He draws in his breath.

COSTAS   But I don't ask you to foak. I ask you come with brother's boat. Different thing. Boat ees boat – foak ees foak.

DOUGIE *and* JEANETTE *walk forward and into the gate towards hotel.*

DOUGIE   Absolutely bloody charming!

They disappear into the hotel. SHIRLEY *is embarrassed, but amused.* COSTAS *continues talking, unperturbed.*

COSTAS   Shall I come eh tomorrow nine o'clock em? I breeng food, I breeng wine and we go. Eh tomorrow um I just make you happy. No need be sad. You no need be 'fraid. I geeve word of honour – I don't try make foak weez you.

He looks at SHIRLEY.

COSTAS   Okay?

SHIRLEY *smiling with sudden confidence.*

SHIRLEY   Okay. See you in the morning.

He nods and they shake hands. She turns and walks towards the hotel. He looks after her.

80 *Interior* SHIRLEY'S *hotel bedroom – day*

A typical tourist bedroom. SHIRLEY, *dressed for her day on* COSTAS'S *boat, is sitting at the dressing table, finishing her make-up. There is a knock at the door.*

SHIRLEY (*to herself*) Oh God, he's come up to me room.

She puts down her make-up, gets up and moves towards the door.

SHIRLEY (*calls*) All right. I'm coming.

But before she can reach the door it opens and JANE *appears.* SHIRLEY *looks at* CAMERA, *eyebrows raised as if saying: 'Oh great'.*

JANE Oh – Shirley! – can you forgive me? I've been completely selfish, haven't I? But I'm going to make it up to you.

SHIRLEY *opens her mouth to speak, but* JANE *rushes on.*

JANE Oh come on – say you forgive me. Let's make today the real start of our holiday. I've hired the car. We'll tour the island, stop off and have lunch somewhere nice – just the two of us. Oh Shirley – can you forgive me?

SHIRLEY (*pausing*) 'Course I forgive you.

JANE Oh . . .

She embraces SHIRLEY *warmly.*

JANE I know you must have been having the most awful time. I suppose you've just been sitting here talking to the wall, haven't you? Never mind. I'll do a quick change, and we'll get straight off.

There is a knock at the door. JANE *turns and opens it.* COSTAS *is standing there. He and* JANE *stare at each other.*

JANE Yes, what is it? Room service? Shirley did you order something?

COSTAS *walks straight past* JANE *into the room and confronts* SHIRLEY.

COSTAS Shirley, you come now! You you late! I . . . I . . . I put the eh food, wine on the boat. I wait down, but you don't come. (*he shrugs*) Then I realisation em . . . em Shirley and me, we are eh going bed so late last night, En probably she eh overslept.

SHIRLEY Oh yeah.

COSTAS So em . . . you come now – I eh I wait down. Please . . . please – hurry.

JANE *is still by the door. He turns to her.*

COSTAS Oh I . . . I'm apologise for eh interrupt. You may now continue cleaning room.

JANE *looks at* COSTAS *who smiles. He hurries past her and out, shutting the door after him.* JANE *turns on* SHIRLEY.

JANE (*shocked*) Shirley – what *are* you playing at?

SHIRLEY Me? You're the one who went off with the walking groin.

JANE Now look, Shirley – you've never been abroad before. You don't know what you are doing.

SHIRLEY Jane – he's just a kind man.

JANE (*with a scornful laugh*) Oh, Shirley! Men like that – these Greek Islanders – they're just waiting for bored middle-aged women.

SHIRLEY (*interrupting with great force*) Don't you dare.

JANE'S *jaw drops as* SHIRLEY *passes her and pulls open the door.*

Interior corridor, SHIRLEY'S *hotel – day*

SHIRLEY *comes from her room and starts walking quickly along the corridor.* JANE *appears in the doorway behind her and calls.*

JANE (*off*) Shirley.

SHIRLEY *stops and turns to* JANE *and they both walk along the corridor.*

JANE I just hope you know what you're doing. I hope for your sake you're going to be safe.

SHIRLEY   Oh I'm sure I will. He's a very good sailor.

She doesn't realise that behind her, as she speaks, DOUGIE *and* JEANETTE *are climbing the stairs, carrying equipment for the beach. They hear* SHIRLEY *as she continues talking to* JANE.

SHIRLEY   And anyway he's given me his word of honour that he won't try and make fuck with me.

DOUGIE *and* JEANETTE *look at each other.* SHIRLEY *sees them and stops.*

SHIRLEY (*cordially, as to old friends*)   Dougie – Jeanette! How are you both?

She indicates JANE.

SHIRLEY   This is my friend, Jane. I was just telling her what a marvellous couple you are.

DOUGIE *and* JEANETTE *smirk at* JANE.

SHIRLEY   And you know what she said? She said she'd *love* to spend an hour or two on the beach with you. (*calling back*) Bye . . . Bye Jane.

She hurries past DOUGIE *and* JEANETTE *and on along the corridor.* DOUGIE *and* JEANETTE *move to* JANE.

JEANETTE   Well, we *were* just off to the beach actually.
DOUGIE   You come with us love – you're more than welcome.

JEANETTE *laughs and walks out followed by* DOUGIE. JANE *follows them, tightlipped with anger.*

82 *Exterior harbour – day*

In a long shot, we see COSTAS'S *boat heading out to sea.*

83 *Exterior* COSTAS'S *boat at sea – day*

SHIRLEY *is steering the boat, concentrating, excited as the craft ploughs through the water.*

SHIRLEY   I'm steering the boat, you know.

COSTAS *walks from bow of boat and sits beside her.*

COSTAS   Shall we try to pass in this direction . . . Eh there we are going to find eh a small bay. Hm . . very beautiful – Ho Ho Ho Ho. There we are going to feesh, eh we eat, drink, talk.

He gestures ahead and places his hand over SHIRLEY'S *hand on the tiller. She withdraws her hand.*

84 *Exterior sea – day*

A long shot of COSTAS'S *boat heading towards a secluded bay on the island.* COSTAS *is now at the tiller.*

85 *Exterior small bay – day*

COSTAS'S *boat is anchored some way off-shore in a secluded bay.*

86 *Exterior* COSTAS'S *boat – day*

The remains of a picnic meal is on the cabin roof. SHIRLEY *and* COSTAS *are sitting on the side of the boat, with their feet almost dangling in the water. They are laughing together at something that's just been said.*

COSTAS   But with the rope you know I mean . . .

They both laugh, SHIRLEY *throws pieces of bread into the sea.*

SHIRLEY *(suddenly looking at him)*   What is it with you Costas?
COSTAS   No I don't eh.
SHIRLEY   You really know how to talk with women don't you?
COSTAS   Well I . . . well.
SHIRLEY   I mean most fellas y' know they've got no idea of how to talk to a woman.
COSTAS   No?
SHIRLEY   No.
COSTAS   Hmm.

SHIRLEY   They feel they have to take over the conversation. You know – if you say something like, like 'My favourite season is the autumn', they go 'Oh, oh. *My* favourite season's spring.' And then you have ten minutes of them talking about why they like spring. And you weren't talking about spring you were talking about autumn – so what do you do? Talk about what they want to talk about . . . . you don't talk at all. Or you wind up talking to yourself.

We see COSTAS *from* SHIRLEY'S *point of view as she continues:*

SHIRLEY   You don't do that.
COSTAS   Well, I eh, I just like listen – also look.

She smiles.

COSTAS   Hm for you . . . I am, I happy.

He raises his wine glass and drinks. She indicates the water.

SHIRLEY   Hey Costas. How deep do you think it is down there?
COSTAS   Oh maybe a thousand metres.
SHIRLEY   Go 'way!
COSTAS (*with a shrug*)   Hm, maybe eh maybe ten thousand. Who knows? Hm, maybe, maybe so deep, it goes on forever.
SHIRLEY   I wanna jump in.
COSTAS   You want to swim?

SHIRLEY *points up to the roof of the cabin.*

SHIRLEY   I wanna jump off the roof!
COSTAS (*laughing*)   I eh theenk um Shirley Valentine is um a bit crazy.
SHIRLEY   Costas – Shirley Valentine is loop the bloody loop!
COSTAS   Loop the *bloody* loop!
SHIRLEY   The only thing is I . . . I . . . I . . . haven't got my cossie on.
COSTAS   It's not possible to swim . . .

SHIRLEY *mimes swimming costume.*

SHIRLEY Swimming costume.

COSTAS *lifts his arms in a wide gesture of amusement.*

COSTAS Aah!

He starts to take his clothes off. With a happy grin, so does SHIRLEY.

87 *Exterior small bay – day*

In a long shot from a distance, we see the nude figures of COSTAS *and* SHIRLEY *clamber on the side of the boat and dive in.* CAMERA *tilts down with* SHIRLEY *as she disappears under the sea then surfaces.*

COSTAS *surfaces. Then we see them revelling in the warm sea, duck-diving, swimming, paddling, somersaulting.* SHIRLEY *swims into a close shot, with* COSTAS *a little distance away. She floats in the sea.*

SHIRLEY *(VO)* It's marvellous to be with such a good man. I know whatever happens he won't take anything from me. I know he'll keep his promise. But the truth is . . . (SHIRLEY *turns and speaks to the* CAMERA) I don't want him to.

She turns, swims up to COSTAS *and puts her arms round his neck. He turns and holds her. They look at each other, smiling a little. Then, gently they kiss.*

88 *Exterior boat – day*

SHIRLEY *and* COSTAS *lie on a towel kissing. But rather than moving up to witness what's happening on deck, the* CAMERA *dips to the water line as waves begin to lap the hull and the boat begins to gently rock in the water. We hear the great swell of a symphony orchestra rising in scale and crescendo. The sea washes the beach. The flag flies at the top of the mast.*

The boat rocks more and the waves lap. We focus on SHIRLEY *and* COSTAS *again as the music abruptly stops.*

SHIRLEY Oh my God, where did that orchestra come from?

COSTAS *bends down and kisses* SHIRLEY'S *breast, then moves down her body and out of frame.*

SHIRLEY   Oh.

SHIRLEY *sits up. She turns, conspiratorially, to the* CAMERA *and speaks directly to it.*

SHIRLEY (*quietly*)   He kissed me stretch marks y' know.

COSTAS *rises up. She looks at him.*

SHIRLEY   You kissed my stretch marks.
COSTAS   Now don't, don't be too stupid to try and hide these lines. They, they are lovely because they are part of you and you are lovely. So, don't hide, 'em, don't hide.

We see SHIRLEY *beginning to be carried away by this.*

COSTAS   Be proud. Show em – These, these marks, show that, eh that you are alive, that you survive. Don't try to hide these lines. They are the marks of life.

SHIRLEY *is looking deeply into his eyes before turning to look over his shoulder and straight into* CAMERA.

SHIRLEY (*to* CAMERA)   Aren't men full of shit?

89 *Exterior sea – day (evening)*

A long shot of COSTAS'S *boat chugging along slowly silhouetted against the setting sun. The* CAMERA *tracks in and we see* SHIRLEY *sitting on the prow of the boat and* COSTAS *inside the cabin steering.*

SHIRLEY   I think I've fallen in love.

90 *Exterior cove – day*

This is SHIRLEY'S *cove, where she talks to the* ROCK. *Now, she and* JANE *are sitting on the* ROCK *wearing swimsuits.*

JANE   Oh, for God's sake, Shirley – you're acting like a stupid teenager. I suppose the next thing you're going to tell me was that the earth moved.

SHIRLEY   Jane – I thought there'd been an earthquake.

JANE   Oh! Spare me the details – please!

JANE *gets to her feet angrily. She walks quickly towards the sea.* SHIRLEY *follows after her.*

SHIRLEY   Oh listen Jane, listen. I . . . I haven't fallen in love with him. It, it . . . was sweet. It was a day full of kindness. But I haven't fallen in love with him.

JANE   Hmph.

JANE *walks off.* SHIRLEY *talks to herself.*

SHIRLEY   Well I haven't fallen in love with him. I've fallen in love with the idea of living.

91 *Interior* SHIRLEY'S *kitchen – night*

JOE *is sitting amongst the remnants of beer bottles and overflowing ashtrays.*

JOE   Why? Why did she have to do this to me? If she wanted to go on holiday all she had to do was ask. I would have let her go. I mean there was no need for deceit. I mean I may not be the best husband in the world Wall, but I love her. I do love her. Honest.

92 *Exterior village street – day*

A quiet side street of small white houses. A flower seller stands behind a donkey piled with flowers. SHIRLEY *stands admiring the profusion of flowers, then walks forward.*

FLOWER SELLER   The flowers.

SHIRLEY (*in Greek*)   Orea. [beautiful]

The FLOWER SELLER *holds out a bunch of flowers.*

FLOWER SELLER   Is beautiful.
SHIRLEY (*in Greek*)   How . . . how much is these flowers?

FLOWER SELLER *replies in Greek and* SHIRLEY *hands her a note.*

SHIRLEY   Here you are.
FLOWER SELLER   Thank you very much.

She hands SHIRLEY *a red rose.*

SHIRLEY   Oh, Efchuristo. [Thank you]

She walks on.

93 *Exterior of square – day*

We see a wedding procession, led by a band, followed by the bride and her family including COSTAS, *move across the square.* COSTAS *dances to the band. They move out of the square down a street to the harbour.* COSTAS *turns to a woman beside him.*

COSTAS   Bought yourself a wardrobe.

94 *Exterior café – day*

SHIRLEY *is sitting at a table watching as the procession starts to pass her. The* MUSICIANS, *then* BRIDE *and* BRIDEGROOM, *followed by the* PARENTS, RELATIVES *and* FRIENDS *– all dressed in their best clothes. As* COSTAS *passes* SHIRLEY, *they see each other. He steps aside and leaves the procession, smiling with pleasure he goes to her table.*

COSTAS   Shirley . . . Ah . . . Come, come to join the family! My niece becomes married.
SHIRLEY (*a little doubtful*)   I . . . no, no I . . . I can't, I mean I would be butting in.
COSTAS   Oh come, come you please. I enjoy. It's good. It's good that we meet here.

COSTAS *guides* SHIRLEY *to the procession.*

95 *Exterior church – day*

Wedding procession moves with the priest into the small whitewashed church. The bell tolls on the steeple.

96 *Interior church – day*

The wedding ceremony is in progress. We watch it. SHIRLEY *stands beside* COSTAS *watching and listening with interest and enjoyment, as the priest leads the service then places head dress circlets on the bride and groom which* COSTAS *swaps round. The bride and groom circle round with* COSTAS *holding the circlets. Everyone throws rice and rose petals.*

97 *Interior taverna – day*

The wedding feast is in progress. The BRIDE *and* BRIDEGROOM, PARENTS, RELATIVES *are all enjoying themselves. There is music. The younger people are dancing, the older ones are sitting at long tables eating, drinking, singing.* COSTAS *dances. With the party, but at one end of a table, is* SHIRLEY. *She has a glass of wine and is thoroughly enjoying herself. Clapping along to the music,* COSTAS *moves over to join* SHIRLEY.

COSTAS   You enjoy it?
SHIRLEY   It's wonderful.
COSTAS   Ah. The man standing over there . . .

The rest of his dialogue is drowned by music. A lady in white moves over and pulls COSTAS *up to dance.* SHIRLEY *laughs watching him.*
    She watches the proceedings – the dancing, the laughter, the easy joy of these people. SHIRLEY *smiles again as she watches* COSTAS, *dancing outrageously. She quietly stands, turns and leaves.* COSTAS *stops dancing as he notices* SHIRLEY'S *empty chair. He goes out to look for her.*

98 *Exterior* COSTAS'S *taverna – night*

SHIRLEY *is walking away from the taverna,* COSTAS *appears in the doorway. He sees* SHIRLEY *walking away and calls to her.*

COSTAS   Shirley . . . Shirley.

She turns and waits as he runs up to her.

COSTAS   Where you go? You . . . you . . . you don't like my family, my friends . . .
SHIRLEY   Oh no Costas. They're lovely.
COSTAS   So why, why you go?
SHIRLEY   I just . . . I just wanna be on me own for a bit. Do you understand?
COSTAS   You, you are again sad.
SHIRLEY (*smiling*)   No . . . no, I'm not sad. It's just that I go back home soon.

COSTAS *nods.*

COSTAS   Hmm . . . Back to your own life.
SHIRLEY   Yeah.

SHIRLEY *points to the taverna.*

SHIRLEY   Go on, go go back to . . . . They're all waitin' for you.
COSTAS   Why I'll see you tomorrow?
SHIRLEY   Yeh . . . see you tomorrow.

SHIRLEY *walks away and we hold* COSTAS *as he watches* SHIRLEY *walking away.*

99 *Exterior hotel – night*

SHIRLEY *walks towards the hotel. She turns and looks back to the taverna. We hear* SHIRLEY *in voice over.*

SHIRLEY (*VO*)   I've got this thought in me head.

She turns and walks away to the hotel.

SHIRLEY   This shocking thought. And it wouldn't go away.

She stops and leans against the wall.

SHIRLEY   I keep trying to think of other things to make this thought go away. But it wouldn't. It's always there in me head.

100   *Interior COSTAS'S taverna – night*

SHIRLEY *is sitting on a bar stool. At one of the tables* COSTAS *is playing the guitar quietly, as much for himself as for the one or two* CUSTOMERS. SHIRLEY *is locked in thought. We hear her voice over.*

SHIRLEY (*VO*)   If . . . if for some reason, I didn't go back . . . home . . . Who . . . would miss me?

SHIRLEY *ponders this proposition as behind her two* GERMAN CUSTOMERS *enter.*
   The CUSTOMERS *mistake* SHIRLEY *for the waitress.*

CUSTOMER   Zwei cafes, bitte.
SHIRLEY   Eh?
WOMAN   Two coffees, please.
SHIRLEY   Oh. Yeah yeah. Two coffees. Right.

SHIRLEY *begins to prepare the coffee. She is still deep in thought. As she prepares the coffee she turns and addresses the* WALL *as she once did in her own kitchen.*

SHIRLEY   I mean . . . look, if I didn't go back . . . who would really care? I mean, they'd notice that I wasn't there. But they wouldn't really miss me. Would they?

We see the GERMAN CUSTOMERS *look at each other, wondering what planet this woman is from.*

SHIRLEY   Why should I go back to being that woman?

The GERMAN CUSTOMERS *leave walking past* COSTAS.

SHIRLEY   When that woman isn't needed anymore. I've done me job. There's nothing else for me to do.

COSTAS *looks puzzled, strains to see who* SHIRLEY *is talking to.* SHIRLEY *turns with two cups of coffee for the* CUSTOMERS, *sees they have gone.*

SHIRLEY   Oh!

COSTAS *confronts her.*

COSTAS   Shirley. Who are you talk to?
SHIRLEY   The wall, Costas – just the wall.

She beams him a big smile as she presents him a coffee.

COSTAS   My God!

101   *Exterior seafront restaurant, Little Venice – day.*

SHIRLEY   *and*   JANE *at restaurant table.* JANE *tries to attract the* WAITER'S *attention.*

JANE   Excuse me signore.
SHIRLEY   I'm serious Jane, I mean it.
JANE   (*impatiently*)   Oh, for God's sake – what about your children for a start?

As SHIRLEY *talks,* JANE *only half-listens, trying to attract the attention of a* WAITER.

SHIRLEY   What about them? They've grown up. Jane, I've spent twenty odd years rearin' them, lookin' after them till they were old enough to make their own way. An' they have. They've gone. (*She thinks for a moment. Then . . .*) No, I mean they'll say it's awful, they'll say it's terrible to have a mother who went on holiday an' didn't come back. They'll get over it. I mean – would it cause anyone any real sufferin' if I didn't go home?

JANE *is trying to catch the eye of the* WAITER.

SHIRLEY   Would it, Jane?
JANE   Shirley . . . every year millions and millions of people go on holiday – and every year those same millions and millions

76

of people have such a good time that they don't want to go back.

SHIRLEY   Yeh, but just supposing.

JANE   And that's all there is to it.

WAITER *moves to her.*

JANE   And, if you don't mind, Shirley, I'm trying to order lunch.

She opens the menu.

JANE   Can we have two greek salads please? And stuffed tomatoes.

SHIRLEY   Yeh.

WAITER   Yes.

SHIRLEY   And a Moussaka special – yes – Moussaka special. And one lamb and green beans.

SHIRLEY (*to Jane*)   Yes.

JANE *continues ordering inaudibly in the background.*

SHIRLEY (*resigned*)   Because we don't do what we want to do – do we? We do what we have to do an' pretend that's what we want to do. An' what I want to do is stay here – stay here happy Shirley Valentine. But what I have to do is go back. Back to bein' St Joan of the Fitted Units.

102 *Exterior hotel – day*

A coach is parked outside the main entrance to the hotel. The TOURISTS *are boarding – among them we see* DOUGIE *and* JEANETTE, SYDNEY, THELMA *and their two* CHILDREN *and others of the Thikos contingent. All the* TOURISTS *are very sunburnt and a number of them are wearing a variety of holiday hats and garments bought locally.*

JANE *is left standing holding her luggage. She looks around for* SHIRLEY, *then seeing her standing outside the hotel shouts across.*

JANE   Shirley, come *on*! It's just going!

We see SHIRLEY *with* RENOS.

77

SHIRLEY   I'm coming.

SHIRLEY *turns to* RENOS *and holds out her hands.* RENOS *takes them.*

SHIRLEY   Goodbye, Renos – thanks.
RENOS   Madame – you come back next year, I hope.
SHIRLEY   Oh Renos I hope.
RENOS   Kalo taksithi, madame. [Bon voyage]

RENOS *holds on to* SHIRLEY'S *hand.*

SHIRLEY   Efharisto, Renos, Herete. [Thank you, Renos, Good-bye]
JANE   Shirley, your bags are on board. Come on.

JANE *turns away and starts to move towards the coach.* SHIRLEY *lets go of* RENOS'S *hand and starts to follow* JANE. COSTAS *appears from behind her.*

COSTAS   Shirley . . . Shirley.

SHIRLEY *turns and sees* COSTAS *standing behind her.*

SHIRLEY   Costas – we said goodbye . . .
COSTAS   Yes, but em (*a smile and a shrug*) I am here . . . So – goodbye, Shirley. Goodbye, Shirley Valentine.
SHIRLEY   See you Costas.
COSTAS   Mm.

SHIRLEY *shakes her head.*

SHIRLEY   Oh.
COSTAS   Oh.

COSTAS *moves towards her. They embrace then part as the sound of the coach starting up is heard.* SHIRLEY *turns and climbs into the coach, the coach moves away. He raises his hand and waves.*

103 *Interior coach – day*

SHIRLEY *is sitting beside* JANE. *She turns to look at* COSTAS *then looks straight ahead stony-faced.*

104 *Interior airport concourse – day*

The TOURISTS *are queuing up at the check-in desk. Among them we see* DOUGIE *and* JEANETTE, SYDNEY *and* THELMA *and their two* CHILDREN *and others of the Thikos party.*

SHIRLEY, *carrying her shoulder bag, and* JANE *are just loading their luggage from a trolley on to the platform beside the* CHECK-IN CLERK. *We see one of* SHIRLEY'S *cases with a label marked 'S. Bradshaw, Manchester Airport, England', being carried by the porter to the conveyer belt.*

SHIRLEY *watches her suitcase as it begins its journey along the conveyer belt. She watches it until it disappears through the rubber flaps.* SHIRLEY *looks at* JANE *who is dealing with the* CHECK-IN CLERK.

The CHECK-IN CLERK *hands* JANE *the tickets. The bags have now all gone through.* JANE *turns, tickets in hand.*

JANE   Right then.

She exits, but SHIRLEY *does not follow her. She stands facing the* CAMERA.

ANNOUNCER (*VO Tannoy*)   Your attention please. This is the last call for Olympic Airways Flight 259 to Manchester.

JANE *moves with her hand luggage to the security check.*

ANNOUNCER (*VO Tannoy*)   Closing now at Gate No. 1.

SHIRLEY *stands amongst passengers. Then suddenly she turns and walks away.*

JANE (*calls*)   Shirley.

JANE *standing amongst passengers with* DOUGIE *and* JEANETTE *behind her realises* SHIRLEY *isn't amongst them. From* JANE'S *point of view, we see* SHIRLEY *walking steadily away towards the exit.*

JANE   Shirley! . . . Shirley, where are you going? Shirley . . . !

In a close shot, SHIRLEY *reaches the exit. The automatic doors open. For an instant she pauses. Then, calmly and confidently, without a backward glance, she walks out into the sunshine.*

JANE *turns to* DOUGIE *and* JEANETTE.

JANE   She's gone.
JEANETTE   What do you expect?
DOUGIE   Yes, what?

105 *Exterior* COSTAS'S *taverna* – *day*

SHIRLEY *walks along the road to the* TAVERNA *with her case.*

106 *Interior taverna veranda* – *day*

SHIRLEY *walks across the veranda, case in hand.*

COSTAS (*off to woman*)   Eh tomorrow we take my brother's boat
– we go all round the island.

We see COSTAS *at the bar talking to a good looking woman in her early forties.*

COSTAS   You afraid?

WOMAN *shakes her head.*

COSTAS   Ay . . . afraid I won't to make foak with you.
WOMAN   What?
COSTAS   But, I don't ask to try to make foak weez you, I ask
to come my brother's boat. Ees . . . Ees different thing. Boat
ees boat – (*he sees* SHIRLEY) – and foak is . . .

SHIRLEY *smiles.*

COSTAS (*to woman*)   Oh my goodness, eh. Excuse me for one
moment.

As he comes round the bar towards SHIRLEY, *she moves away. He comes
to her, startled.*

SHIRLEY (*smiling*)   It's all right Costas – you don't have to
worry.
COSTAS   But did you lose the plane?

He takes her arm and hurriedly guides her to a table. She sits.

SHIRLEY Don't worry Costas. I haven't come back for you.
I've come back for a job – the job in this taverna.

COSTAS (*realising*) A job! You, you want to work here?

SHIRLEY Yes, why not? I mean this place could do with someone to sort it out – I mean, given the amount of time you
spend on your brother's boat.

She smiles. COSTAS *smiles – sheepish but relieved.*

107 *Interior arrivals concourse Manchester Airport – night*

TOURISTS *are coming through from Customs, wheeling their trolley loads
of luggage. Among them we see* DOUGIE *and* JEANETTE, SYDNEY *and*
THELMA *with their* CHILDREN *and others of the Thikos contingent. Some
are greeted by waiting* RELATIVES *and* FRIENDS. *Now among those waiting, we see* JOE *who is mostly hidden behind a vast bouquet of flowers.
Now, from Customs,* JANE *appears, pushing a loaded trolley with her
luggage and* SHIRLEY'S. *She comes forward to* JOE. *He is looking beyond
her for* SHIRLEY *and doesn't see* JANE *until she stops in front of him and,
without speaking, pulls* SHIRLEY'S *suitcase from the trolley, dumps it at
his feet and goes on her way, leaving him open-mouthed, staring from the
suitcase to her receding figure and then at the suitcase again.* JOE *looks
after her, then down at* SHIRLEY'S *suitcase.*

108 *Interior taverna – SHIRLEY'S bedroom – day*

SHIRLEY *gets out of bed and puts on her dressing gown. We see from her
point of view the stunning view of the sea.*

109 *Interior/exterior COSTAS'S taverna – day*

We follow SHIRLEY *as she moves into the taverna. We hear the phone
ring and stay with* SHIRLEY *as* COSTAS *answers it.*

COSTAS (*off*) Yes . . . oh.

COSTAS Shirley. Someone wants to see you on the telephone.

SHIRLEY *picks up the receiver.*

SHIRLEY   Hello.

We hear JOE *shouting down the phone.*

JOE   You're a disgrace.

110 *Interior* SHIRLEY'S *kitchen – day*

We see JOE *pacing around the pristine kitchen, phone in hand.*

JOE (*into phone*)   A bloody disgrace – to . . . to . . . to the children – to me – to yourself. I'm a laughing stock! That's what I am, a laughing stock.

111 *Interior* COSTAS'S *taverna – day*

In a corner, behind the bar SHIRLEY *is on the phone. Behind her, we see there are* CUSTOMERS *sitting on stools at the bar and at tables out on the terrace.*

SHIRLEY (*into phone*)   Listen, um, Joe – I can't talk now. I'm busy.
JOE (*VO from phone*)   You're busy doing what? What're you doing?
SHIRLEY (*into phone*)   I'm workin'. D'you understand.

112 *Interior* SHIRLEY'S *kitchen – day*

JOE *is shouting at the top of his voice.*

JOE (*on phone*)   No, I bloody don't understand. I've taken time off work because of you.

113 *Interior* COSTAS'S *taverna – day*

SHIRLEY *with phone to ear listens to* JOE *continuing to harangue her.*

JOE (*VO*)   Stop this arsin' around, and get yourself back home.

114 *Interior* SHIRLEY'S *kitchen – day*

JOE I've had just about enough.

He stops as he hears the phone being hung up – we hear the dialling tone.

JOE · Hello! . . . Shirley? Shirley? Are you there? (*he rattles the receiver furiously*)

He slams the receiver down, crashes his fist down on the phone, then grabs the cable and rips it from the wall.

115 *Exterior* COSTAS'S *taverna – day*

Business is brisk. At one table two holiday-makers – a LONDONER *and his* WIFE *– are studying the menu with puzzled frowns.* SHIRLEY *comes to them.*

LONDONER Er – miss – er – what's this klef – er . . . ?
SHIRLEY Kleftika. It's very nice.
WIFE Oh – you're English.
LONDONER Oh, what a relief. Well, what *is* this – klef . . . klef . . .?
SHIRLEY Kleftika. Oh it's lovely. Lamb cooked very, very slowly with oregano.
WIFE (*shaking her head*) No – I don't think so.
LONDONER (*studying the menu*) Well – it's a bit – eh . . . eh . . .
SHIRLEY I tell you what. Listen, eh, it's not on the menu – but – would you like me to do you both some chips an' egg?
WIFE (*brightening*) Ooh, yes.
LONDONER Smashing!
SHIRLEY Right.

As SHIRLEY *turns to go into the taverna, she looks at the* CAMERA, *smiles and winks.*

116 *Interior office in builder's yard*

We see JOE *on the telephone.*

JOE (*into phone*)   I'm phonin' from work because our phone's out of order – that's why. It's costing me a bleedin' fortune this time of the day. Now listen to me Shirl.

117 *Exterior road, Mykonos – day*

SHIRLEY *is riding along the road on a motor cycle as we hear* JOE'S *phone call continue over.*

JOE (*over phone*)   You belong back here. Don't put the phone down – don't. Hello – Shirley – Now listen . . . now Jane's told me all about it, you know em about em . . .

118 *Exterior open air market, Mykonos – day*

SHIRLEY *stops at a fish stall.*

JOE (*over phone*)   About you makin' a fool of yourself with this holiday romance thing.

We hear SHIRLEY'S *voice on the other end of the phone.*

SHIRLEY (*over phone*)   No, no, Joe – you've got it all wrong . . .

JOE (*over phone*)   Look, oh, oh. Okay, now all right it happens. Okay, middle aged women make fools of themselves when they go abroad. But look I am prepared to forgive you. If you're prepared to promise.

119 *Interior office in builder's yard – day*

JOE (*on phone*)   That you'll get yourself on a plane and get yourself back home.

120 *Interior* COSTAS'S *taverna – day*

We see SHIRLEY *with the phone to her ear.*

SHIRLEY (*on phone*)   Hey, Joe will you listen for one moment, will you just listen. The only holiday romance I've had is with meself. An . . . an' I think I've come to like meself really.

(Over the following scene, we continue to hear SHIRLEY'S *voice overlaid.)*

121 *Exterior open air market – day*

A small market – stalls of flowers, fruit and vegetables, etc. The market is busy with housewives and other shoppers.

SHIRLEY *is at one of the fruit and vegetable stalls, busily buying supplies for the taverna. She has her phrase book in her hand to help her as she bargains with the* STALL-HOLDER. *With her well-tanned skin, she looks a picture of health and happiness.*

SHIRLEY *(VO) (continuing)* I think I'm all right. I think that if I saw myself now I'd say – 'that woman's okay'.

JOE *(VO)* But, Shirley – you can't just run away from life.

SHIRLEY *(VO)* That's right, Joe. I agree with you. And now that I've found some life, I've no intention of runnin' away from it.

JOE *(VO)* But you belong back here.

SHIRLEY *(VO)* Please Joe, it's no good to keep phonin' . . .

122 *Interior* COSTAS'S *taverna – night*

We see SHIRLEY *on the taverna phone.*

SHIRLEY *(on phone)* . . . because I'm not comin' back. Can't you understand. I am not comin' home.

123 *Interior call box – night*

JOE *(on phone)* But Shirley, don't you understand love? You don't know what you're sayin' because you're goin' through the change of life.

124 *Interior* COSTAS'S *taverna – night*

SHIRLEY *(on phone)* That's right, Joe. That's exactly what it is, Joe. It's a change of life.

125 *Interior office in builder's yard – day*

JOE *enters the office and walks past* BRIAN *to the filing cabinet.*

BRIAN   Why don't you go and see her Dad?

JOE *walks to his desk and sits down.*

JOE   She's in Greece. She's not down the soddin' road.
BRIAN   So? Go to Greece.
JOE   Go to Greece! I've got a business to run.
BRIAN   What is it with people when they get old?
JOE   Old – Who's old? I'm only in me forties.
BRIAN   Yeah I know. But you're frightened aren't you?
JOE   Frightened of what?
BRIAN   You're frightened of anythin' that's different Dad.

JOE *leans back in his chair and crosses his arms.*

BRIAN   I used to like you. I did. You were great y' know. You used to laugh. You used to talk to us all. You've not half become a borin' bastard.

He turns away and JOE *watches him.*

126 *Interior COSTAS'S taverna – day*

On the veranda of the taverna, a couple of tables are occupied by HOLIDAYMAKERS *drinking coffee or Coca-cola.*
   SHIRLEY *carrying two loaded shopping baskets, comes along.*

JULIE   Oh here she is.
SHIRLEY   Chips an' egg.
JOHN   Nice Shirley.

127 *Interior back of taverna – day*

COSTAS *is sitting at a table reading a newspaper.* SHIRLEY *puts her shopping down.*

SHIRLEY   Yassu Costas.

COSTAS   Yassu Shirley.

COSTAS   Hey, come for you one telegram.

SHIRLEY   Oh.

SHIRLEY, *concerned, opens the telegram and reads it.*

COSTAS (*anxiously*)   Is bad news?

SHIRLEY *smiles, an amused, rueful smile.*

SHIRLEY   No – No. Not really. It's from Joe.

COSTAS   Well.

SHIRLEY   He's comin' to fetch me, to take me back home – God love him, he must have been watchin' Rambo.

She looks down at the telegram.

COSTAS (*taken aback*)   Come. Your Joe is comes here?

SHIRLEY   Yeah.

COSTAS   When . . . when he come?

SHIRLEY   Er – Friday.

COSTAS   Friday – is that tomorrow Friday?

SHIRLEY   Yeah.

COSTAS   Shrr that's . . . oh it's a pity because . . . um I receive a telephone call. I must go to Athens. Eh my sister – is sick, em – she she wants me to . . . to be.

SHIRLEY *shrugs.*

COSTAS   So . . . I shall.

COSTAS *shrugs.*

COSTAS   You understand, Shirley.

SHIRLEY (*her eyes twinkling*)   Oh, yes Costas – of course I understand.

128 *Exterior COSTAS'S taverna and sea wall – day (evening)*

A couple of HOLIDAYMAKERS have just finished their drinks. They are the only customers. SHIRLEY comes out from the bar as they get up. They call goodnight to her.

JULIE Goodnight Shirley.

SHIRLEY Goodnight Julie, goodnight John.

JOHN Goodnight.

SHIRLEY *is carrying a carafe of wine and two glasses. From* SHIRLEY'S *point of view, we see that by the sea wall is a table and chairs, placed where* COSTAS *had put them for her on her first visit to the taverna.*

129 *Exterior Mykonos, dusty hotel road – evening*

In the distance – we see a man on foot, carrying a suitcase, hot and tired. As he approaches, dressed unsuitably in a blue lounge suit and tie, we see it is JOE. *He switches his heavy case to his other hand.*

130 *Exterior* COSTAS'S *taverna and sea wall – evening*

SHIRLEY *is sitting at the table – she pours wine in a glass. Then puts on dark glasses. The sun is low on the horizon, almost touching the sea.*

131 *Exterior hotel road – evening*

JOE *is sat on his case. He wipes the sweat from his brow. He looks down towards the bay where he sees a woman (*SHIRLEY*) sitting by a table at the edge of the sea.* JOE *registers her, displaying obvious male approval.*

132 *Exterior* COSTAS'S *taverna and sea wall – evening*

SHIRLEY *is sitting at the table. She pours herself a glass of wine. She is relaxed and peaceful. She turns and sees, in the distance, the figure of* JOE *walking towards the bay. She takes off her dark glasses.*

SHIRLEY (*in the presence of the* CAMERA) Oh I hope he stays for a while. He needs a holiday. He needs to feel the sun on his skin and to be in water that's as deep as forever.

JOE *walks towards the taverna.* SHIRLEY *puts her dark glasses on again.* JOE *walks along.*

SHIRLEY *sits at ease, sipping her wine, watching* JOE *approach.*

Now JOE *is quite near. He is looking about him with casual interest. As he reaches* SHIRLEY *she looks up at him. He looks back at her with a glint of male interest in his eyes. She smiles – a tentative smile. He looks away and walks on past her.* SHIRLEY *looks at the* CAMERA *as if to say 'typical'. She calls out to him.*

SHIRLEY Joe.

He stops, turns slowly and looks at her. He takes a pace or two towards her. She takes off her dark glasses. He puts his case down.

JOE (*shaking his head in wonder*) I didn't recognise you.
SHIRLEY (*smiling a welcome*) Hello. I used to be the mother. I used to be the wife. But now I'm Shirley Valentine again.

JOE *looks at her.*

SHIRLEY Would you like to join me for a drink?
JOE Er . . . thanks.

He sits beside SHIRLEY, *looking at her – puzzled, curious. She pours wine into his glass, refills her own.*
    The CAMERA *pulls back as they pick up their glasses and silently toast each other. Then as the* CAMERA *continues to pull back, up and away, we see* JOE *lean forward and start talking to* SHIRLEY. *A moment and she smiles, shakes her head – another moment, she nods – another moment, she shakes her head again. The* CAMERA *pulls up and away as* SHIRLEY *and* JOE, *talking and sipping their wine, become distant shadows as the* CAMERA *pulls back to reveal the setting sun.*

▨ Glossary: reading the text

3 *Eleventh Commandment*   Shirley is making fun of the biblical Ten Commandments declared by Moses.

   bragger   boaster.

5 *vegans*   strict vegetarians.

6 *forlornly*   sadly.

8 *clitoris*   sensitive part of the female genitalia.

10 *Kirkby*   district of Liverpool.

   Beirut   capital city of Lebanon, the scene of much warfare in recent years.

   Woolton, Childwall   smart suburbs of Liverpool.

11 *busker poet*   poet making money by performing in public places, such as outside theatres.

   reminiscently   fondly remembering.

12 *emulsion*   paint.

13 *retaliates*   fights back.

15 *palate*   roof of the mouth.

16 *feminist*   woman who believes in equal rights for women.

17 *Cosmopolitan*   monthly magazine published around the world in different languages, regularly including articles about women's issues.

19 *Chester*   Roman city of great historical interest, about 20 miles from Liverpool.

20 *insular*   inward looking, unadventurous.

   prerogative   right.

   demented   mad.

22 *serried ranks*   close-packed rows.

   elocuted   coached in the art of public speaking.

23 *Sputnik*   Russian spaceship.

24 *OBE*   Order of the British Empire, awarded by the Queen for services to others.

25 *exude boredom out of every pore*   act bored with everything and everyone.

26 *irrits*   (slang) irritates me.

31 *mare*   female horse (used as alternative to 'cow').

39 *taramasalata*   a pink fish paté.

48 *caressing*   stroking gently.

---

1   What picture is created of the neighbourhood in which Shirley and Joe live? What techniques of comedy writing – for example, reference to 'the vegetarian bloodhound' – does the writer employ to highlight the characters and attitudes of the neighbours?

2   What changes in Shirley and Joe's married life are summed up in this first part of the screenplay? Again, how does comedy emphasise both the funny and sad sides of their relationship?

3   What words would you use to describe Shirley's emotional state as she leaves for Greece?

4   What role in the drama has been played by the two teenage children?

5   What are your predictions for the way the screenplay will develop and conclude?

---

49 *conspicuous*   attracting attention.

50 *entranced*   fascinated.

    revelation   secret information.

51 *Mykonos*   one of the many Greek islands favoured by tourists.

52 *conspiratorially*   as though making secret plans.

    Lloret, Majorca   Spanish holiday resorts, popular with British tourists.

    crematorium   building in which corpses are cremated.

    dubious   doubtful.

53 *serenely*   calmly.

54 *calamaris*   fried squid, speciality of the region.

    Bon appetit   'happy eating'.

55 *jacuzzi*   a whirlpool bath; Dougie would think it very impressive to say he owns a jacuzzi.

   Michael Caine   British film actor, starred in the film *Educating Rita*.

56 *M.F.I.*   a furniture store trade name.

57 *servility*   acting like a slave.

58 *Kalinikhti*   (Greek) good night.

63 *unperturbed*   unworried.

66 *cordially*   warmly.

68 *cossie*   swimming costume.

75 *proposition*   idea.

77 *inaudibly*   unheard.

   St Joan   the French girl who was burned at the stake for her strong beliefs.

   contingent   group.

79 *Bradshaw*   Shirley's married name is used on the suitcase.

82 *pristine*   very clean and new-looking.

   harangue   to speak to angrily.

87 *rueful*   feeling pity.

   Rambo   a film character, known for his daring deeds and 'macho' behaviour.

89 *tentative*   hesitant.

---

1   Which aspects of the British on holiday abroad does Willy Russell focus on and caricature in the Greek scenes?

2   Does Costas appear to you as anything other than a 'cardboard character', a stereotype of the Greek sailor 'looking for a good time'?

3   During the scenes on the telephone between Shirley and Joe, which character do you sympathise with? Give your reasons.

4   How does Shirley feel at the end about Joe coming out to join her? Are there any lines which suggest that she does or she doesn't want him to come to Mykonos?

5   Do you find the screenplay's conclusion satisfying? Predictable? Disappointing? State your feelings and give reasons.

Study programme

Characters

In fiction it is always important to remember that a writer may well 'load the dice' about a character's personality and attitudes. In shaping your views about a character, consider:

- what the character *does*, and how s/he behaves towards others and in different situations;
- what the character *says*, when and to whom;
- what *others* say about the character.

Shirley Valentine

1. Look back through the screenplay and make a list of the different emotions that you would judge Shirley experiences. Use a thesaurus to extend your vocabulary.

2. Imagine you were at school with Shirley. Write a short description of her, as you remember her, looking back ten years.

3. If you were to talk with the following people, what phrases would they use to describe Shirley's actions in the course of *Shirley Valentine*?

   - Joe
   - Gillian
   - Costas
   - Millandra
   - Marjorie Majors
   - Jane.

4. Compile a selection of lines spoken by Shirley in the screenplay which show her to be:
   - motherly
   - optimistic
   - sad and full of regrets
   - self-sufficient.

5. Using any of the information you have gathered from the above assignments, draft a 500-word character study of Shirley Valentine. Show it to another student for comment, then redraft.

Joe

6. 'You're frightened of anythin' that's different Dad.' To what extent do these words from Brian (page 86) sum up Joe and his views on life?

7. How do you think Joe is seen as a person by:
   - his workmates
   - Gillian
   - Millandra?

8. Look back carefully through the screenplay. Which lines and phrases do you feel best describe:
   - Shirley's feelings about her husband
   - Joe's own feelings about his life
   - Willy Russell's verdict on Joe?

9. Use the textual references you have put together in the above assignments to present a two-minute talk on the subject of Joe Bradshaw and his role in the screenplay.

Other characters

10. What picture do you form of Brian and Millandra from their appearance in

the screenplay? Do they in any way seem to be the children of their parents, in terms of outlook and attitudes?

11 Imagine you are putting together a feature article for a Liverpool newspaper about 'The Mother Who Ran Away to Greece'. You interview Shirley's neighbours and friends. What do they report to you and in what style? Improvise the interviews in small groups. Then write the article.

12 Which of the minor characters do you find believable or convincing? Would you say Willy Russell chooses to caricature any of them for a particular effect?

13 Discuss in groups what you feel the minor characters contribute to the screenplay's comedy and to its underlying themes?

14 Marjorie Majors features strongly in the first part of the screenplay. Why is this? Why does Willy Russell give this character such a profile?

Themes

In common with the great dramatist Bernard Shaw, Willy Russell clearly writes both to entertain and to 'educate'. There are many serious points lying behind the humour.

1 Make a list of lines and incidents in *Shirley Valentine* where the writer is drawing the reader's attention to:
- issues about people's background or class
- people in crisis
- the habits of marriage
- the so-called 'generation gap'
- the 'grass-is-greener' syndrome.

Discuss in groups which of these topics you consider Willy Russell writes most persuasively about?

95

▨ In pairs, improvise an interview with Willy Russell in which you strongly challenge the views he puts across in *Shirley Valentine*. Then write up your interview in a format suitable for publication in a newspaper.

▨ Shirley says:

> *I've lived such a little life. An' even that'll be over pretty soon. I'd allowed myself to live this little life – when inside me there was so much more. An' it's all gone unused. An' now it never will be. Well. Why do we get all this life if we don't ever use it? Why do we all get these ... feelings and dreams and hopes – if we don't ever use them?*

page 61

What seems to be the screenplay's 'message' on the views expressed here by Shirley? Is it true that we all pass 'lives of quiet desperation'? What are your thoughts? Discuss ideas in groups and then mount a whole-class debate on the subject. Think about any plays or novels which you have read that touch upon a similar theme.

▨ Another central issue in the screenplay is concerned with the respective roles of women and men in today's society. Read the following three poems about the position of women, as perceived by female writers.

I Had Rather Be a Woman

I had rather be a woman
Than an earwig
But there's not much in it sometimes.
We both crawl out of bed
But there the likeness ends.
Earwigs don't have to
Feed the children,
Feed the cat,
Feed the rabbits,
Feed the dishwasher.
They don't need
Clean sheets,
Clean clothes,
Clean carpets,

A clean bill of health.
They just rummage about
In chrysanthemums.
No-one expects them
To have their
Teetotal, vegetarian
Mothers-in-law
To stay for Christmas,
Or to feel a secret thrill
At the thought of extending the kitchen.
Earwigs can snap their pincers at life
And scurry about being quite irresponsible.
They enjoy an undeserved reputation
Which frightens the boldest child.
Next time I feel hysterical
I'll bite a hole in a dahlia.

Daphne Schiller

The Washerwoman

She washes her old man's dirty clothes,
her son's dirty clothes,
her daughter's dirty clothes.

Inhumanly clean
like her murdered life
she wipes away at times the sinful tear of a dream
with her clean
washerwoman's hands.

Anna Swir

'Maintenance Engineer'

One Friday night it happened, soon after we were wed,
When my old man came in from work as usual I said:
'Your tea is on the table, clean clothes are on the rack,
Your bath will soon be ready, I'll come up and scrub your back.'
He kissed me very tenderly and said, 'I'll tell you flat
The service I give my machine ain't half as good as that.'
I said ...

97

Chorus

I'm not your little woman, your sweetheart or your dear
I'm a wage slave without wages, I'm a maintenance engineer.

Well then we got to talking. I told him how I felt,
How I keep him running just as smooth as some conveyor belt!
Well after all, it's I'm the one provides the power supply
He goes just like the clappers on me steak'n kidney pie.
His fittings are all shining 'cos I keep 'em nice and clean
And he tells me his machine tool is the best I've ever seen.
But ...

Chorus

The terms of my employment would make your hair turn grey,
I have to be on call you see for 24 hours a day.
I quite enjoy the perks though while I'm working through the night
For we get job satisfaction. Well he does, and then I might.
If I keep up full production, I should have a kid or two,
So some future boss will have a brand new labour force to screw.
So ...

Chorus

The truth began to dawn then, how I keep him fit and trim
So the boss can make a nice fat profit out of me and him.
And, as a solid union man, he got in quite a rage
To think that we're both working hard and getting one man's wage.
I said 'And what about the part-time packing job I do?
That's three men that I work for love, my boss, your boss and you.'
So ...

Chorus

He looked a little sheepish and he said, 'As from today
The lads and me will see what we can do on equal pay.
Would you like a housewives' union? Do you think you should get paid?
As a cook and as a cleaner, as a nurse and as a maid?'
I said, 'Don't jump the gun love, if you did your share at home,
Perhaps I'd have some time to fight some battles of my own.'
For ...

Chorus

I've often heard you tell me how you'll pull the bosses down.
You'll never do it brother while you're bossing me around.
'Til women join the struggle, married, single, white and black
You're fighting with a blindfold and one arm behind your back.
The message has got over now for he's realised at last
That power to the sisters must mean power to the class.
And ...

Chorus

Repeat: I'm not your little woman, your sweetheart or your dear
         I'm a wage-slave without wages
         I'm a maintenance engineer.

Sandra Kerr

What are your reactions to the poems? Which emotions are the writers seeking to stir in their male and female readers? What would Shirley's thoughts be on reading these?

Use the following statements as the basis for discussion or writing:

- Men don't make good 'housewives'.
- Men are men and women are women — they should stick to what they're good at.
- The old order is rapidly changing....

Language and style

▣ The Introduction makes reference to aspects of Willy Russell's writing, in particular his comic touches. Working in small groups, brainstorm a list of words that you would use to describe Russell's style. Then write out the list, heading it with four *key* words or phrases about his style.

▣ What kinds of comedy can be found in *Shirley Valentine*? The following list should help you identify techniques the writer uses:

- *Situation comedy* – a general term meaning comedy based on humorous situations that arise in day-to-day life. For example, where Gillian and Shirley meet unexpectedly in the ladies' underwear department (page 38).

- *Satire* – shows the foolishness (and even evil) of something or someone in an amusing way. For example, Gillian's treatment of her vegetarian bloodhound (page 4).

- *Irony* – linked to satire, this is the sarcastic use of words to imply the opposite of what they normally mean: or irony can refer to a situation where the opposite of what you expect to happen does happen. For example, Shirley says to Jane, 'I was beginning to think you'd fallen down it' (page 50); and young Shirley getting the right answer to the head-mistress's question (page 24).

(Note: 'ironic' and 'sarcastic' are often used to mean the same thing.)

- *Caricature* – this presents a person in a way which exaggerates her or his normal personality and characteristics; for example, the writer's treatment of Sydney and Thelma as British tourists (page 56).

- *Visual humour* – this is action rather than words making us laugh. For example, the paint fight between Shirley and Joe (page 12).

- *Verbal humour* – exchanges of words, one-line quips and jokes between the characters. For example, Shirley says:

  The brown blob on the right of the kitchen is the washin' machine – and the white blob on the left is the cooker. And don't get 'em mixed up, or you might end up with socks on toast!

  page 21

Write down each of these headings on a different sheet of paper. Working in pairs or groups – perhaps each group taking a different kind of comic writing – go through the screenplay noting down as many examples as you can find of situation comedy, satire, visual humour, etc.

Now compare your lists. Are there any lines or incidents that occur under more than one heading? Discuss why that might be.

▨ Using the notes you have gathered for the previous assignment, what statements can you devise which sum up the comic style of Willy Russell? Write an extended essay on this subject, using quotations from *Shirley Valentine* to support your argument.

▨ CAROL *Hey the only thing that trembled for me was the headboard on the bed*   page 9

SHIRLEY *It is! Have you never heard of it? It's called the F Plan!* page 46

SHIRLEY *You go to his villa and enjoy yourself. Give his olives a good pressin'!*   page 51

Jokes about sex and the human body appear regularly in the screenplay. Note down ten examples.

Imagine you are now 'hot-seating' the writer, asking him to justify the inclusion of lines which might cause offence. Working in pairs, improvise the interview. Then write up the dialogue under the title 'The Devil Gets All the Best Lines'!

▨ If you think about comedy in films and on television you will know that sexual matters are the staple diet of many comedy sketches. In groups, discuss:

- examples from current television programmes;
- why the subject of sex attracts comedy writers;
- the difference between laughing at and laughing with;
- whether there are occasions when jokes go too far;
- guidelines you would draw up for writers and broadcasters so that offence is not caused.

▨   'feller'   'friggin''
              'cossie'   'Shirl'

Willy Russell's plays are steeped in the dialect of his native Liverpool. Working with a partner, go through the screenplay noting down as many examples as you can of the Liverpudlian dialect. (Before you begin, check in a dictionary the difference in meaning between 'accent' and 'dialect'.)

Do Shirley and Joe use certain words or phrases regularly in their speech? What about the shape and style of their sentences and their humour?

What statements about the characteristics of the Liverpool dialect can you make? Listening to a Liverpool accent, what do you notice about vowel sounds? (The extracts from *Educating Rita* on pages 110–113 are also worth reading for this assignment.)

Stage and screen

1 This book contains the *screenplay* version of *Shirley Valentine*. The script employs:

- interior/exterior settings
- voice overs
- flashbacks
- camera directions
- camera close-ups and long shots
- rapid cutting from one scene to the next.

How successfully does the writer use these techniques? Why does he use them at certain moments? Refer back to the interview with Willy Russell on pages v–xv. Share your ideas in small groups.

2 An important feature of good comedy writing is that it is almost impossible to make an audience laugh continuously. There have to be quieter moments or 'breathing spaces' in the action. What observations would you make about the structure of *Shirley Valentine*? In groups, discuss the following:

- the number of scenes
- the ordering of the scenes
- the coming and going of the various characters
- the ebb and flow of the action
- the 'Liverpool scenes' versus the 'Greek scenes'
- the busier and quieter moments of the screenplay.

▣ Putting together thoughts and ideas from your discussions above, write a 500-word review of *Shirley Valentine* focusing on its structure on screen. Aim to devote different paragraphs to the points listed above.

▣ *Shirley Valentine* started out as a one-woman stage play in which Shirley delivered a monologue, unbroken except for one interval in the theatre production. The screenplay came second.

Read and study the following two extracts from the original stage play. Read them aloud for best effect.

Then, working in pairs, compare them carefully with the screenplay versions on pages 28 and 82 respectively.

I saw her a few weeks ago, Marjorie Majors. Didn't I wall? I hadn' even heard of her for years. I'm in Town, loaded down with shoppin' an' what's the first thing that always happens when y' in Town loaded down with shoppin'? Right. The heavens opened. An' it's funny the way all these things are linked but they are; once you're in Town, loaded with shoppin' bags, caught in a deluge – it always follows that every bus ever made disappears off the face of the earth. Well I'm standin' there, like a drowned rat, me hair's in ruins an' I've got mascara lines runnin' from my face to me feet, so I thought I might as well trudge up to the Adelphi an' get a taxi. Course when I got there the taxis had gone into hidin' along with the buses. Well I'm just rootin' in me bag, lookin' for somethin' to slash me wrists with when this big white car pulls up to the hotel an' of course I'm standin' right by a puddle an' as the wheels go through it, half the puddle ends up over me an' the other half in me shoppin' bags. Well all I wanted to do by this time was scream. So I did. I just opened me mouth, standin' there in front of the hotel an' let out this scream. I could've been arrested but I didn't care. Well I was in mid scream when I noticed this woman get out the white car an' start comin' towards me. An' she's dead elegant. Know she's walkin' through this torrential rain an' I guarantee not one drop of it was landin' on her. But the second she opened her mouth I knew who she was. I'd recognise those elocution lessons anywhere. 'Forgive me for asking,' she said, 'but didn't you used to be Shirley Valentine?' I just stood there, starin'. And drippin'. 'It is,' she said, 'it's Shirley,' an' the next thing, she's apologisin' for half drownin' me an' she's pullin' me into the hotel an' across the lobby an' into this lounge that's the size of two football pitches. Well, she's ordered tea an' I'm sittin' there, rain water drippin' down me neck an' plastic carrier bags round me feet an' I'm thinkin', *'Well Marjorie, you've waited a long time for your revenge but you've got me in good style now, haven't y'? Well go on, spare me the torture, just put the knife in quick an' let's get it over with; come on tell me all about your bein' an air hostess on Concorde.'* But she didn't say anythin'. She just sat there, lookin' at me, y' know really lookin' at me. I thought I'm not gonna let her milk it so I said, *'You're an' air hostess these days are y' Marjorie? Oh yes, I hear it's marvellous. You travel all over the world don't you?'* But she still just kept lookin' at me. The waitress was just puttin' the tea an' cakes on the table in front of us. I said to her *'This is my friend Marjorie. We were at school together. Marjorie's an air hostess.'* *'An air hostess?,'* Marjorie suddenly said, *'Darling whatever gave you that idea? I certainly travel widely but I'm not an air hostess. Shirley, I'm a hooker. A whore.'* Marjorie Majors – a high class hooker! *'Oh really Marjorie,'* I said, *'An' all that money your mother spent on elocution lessons.'* By this time, the waitress was pourin' the tea into the cream buns! Well me an' Marjorie – God, we had a great afternoon together. She didn't come lordin' it over me at all. Y' know she told me about all the places she works – Bahrain, New York, Munich. An' d' y' know what she told me? When we were at school ... She wanted to be like me. The two of us, sittin' there at the Adelphi, one's like somethin' out of Dynasty, one's like somethin' out the bagwash an' we're havin' a great time confessin' that all those years, we each wanted to be the other. I was sad when I thought about it. Like the two of us could have been great mates – y' know real close. We didn't half get on well together, that afternoon, in the Adelphi. We were rememberin' all kinds. I could've sat there forever – neither of us wanted to leave. But then the time caught up with us an' Marjorie had to get her plane. An' y' know somethin' – she didn't want to go. Paris she had to go to, Paris France, an' she didn't want to. An' an' on the way out ... d' y' know what she did? She leaned forward an' just kissed me – there on the cheek – an' there was real affection in that kiss. It was the sweetest kiss I'd known in years. An' then she, she held my shoulders an' looked at me and said, *'Goodbye Shirley. Goodbye, Shirley Valentine.'*

*

The first time he phoned, y' know after Jane had got back, he screamed at me. He said I must have finally gone mad. He said I was a disgrace – to the Kids, to him, to meself. It was the easiest thing in the world to just put the phone down on him. The second time he phoned he said you can't run away from life. I said I agreed with him an' now I'd found some life I had no intention of runnin' *away* from it. He started to scream an' shout again then; he said he knew all about me 'holiday romance', an' how I'd made a fool of meself but, but if I stopped all this arsin' round, if I got meself on a plane an' got meself home, where I belonged, he said, he said he'd promise never to mention it. I said ... said ... 'The only holiday romance I've had, is with meself Joe. An' ... an' I think ... I've come to like meself, really.' I said to him, I said, 'I think I'm alright Joe. I think that if ... if I saw me, I'd say, that woman's OK....She's alive. She's not remarkable, she's not gonna ... gonna be there in the history books. But she's ... she's there in the time she's livin' in. An' certainly she's got her wounds ... an' her battle scars but maybe, maybe ... a little bit of the bullshit is true an' the wounds shouldn't be hidden away – because, because even the wounds an' the scars are about bein' alive.' There was a long pause. I thought he'd gone off the phone. An' then I heard this voice, 'I knew it,' he was sayin', 'I knew it, it's the bleedin' change of life isn't it?' 'That's right Joe,' I said, 'That's right, it's a change of life. An' that's why you're wastin' your money phonin' me to try an' get me back. I'm not comin' back.' The last time he phoned he said our Brian had been arrested – buskin' without a licence. An' our Millandra was frettin' for me. An' that he loved me an' the only thing he wanted in the world was for me to come back. I explained to him that it was impossible because the woman he wanted to go back didn't exist anymore. An' then I got his letter sayin' he was comin' to get me. To take me back home. Agh, God love him, he must've been watchin' Rambo. He'll be here soon. I hope he stays for a while. He needs a holiday. He needs to feel the sun on his skin an' to be in water that's as deep as forever, an' to have his wet head kissed. He needs to stare out to sea. And to understand. (pause) I asked Costas if he'd put the table out for me again. He said to me 'You look for you dream again?' 'No, Costas,' I said. 'No dream. But I'm gonna sit here an' watch for Joe an' as he walks down the esplanade, an' keeps walkin', because he doesn't recognise me anymore, I'll call out to him. An' as he walks back, an' looks at me, all puzzled an' quizzical, I'll say to him – "Hello. I used to be the mother. I used to be your wife. But now, I'm Shirley Valentine again. Would you like to join me for a drink"?'

Now answer the following questions:

1 Which lines have been lost or edited in the move from stage to screen?

2 Which words and phrases are new in the screenplay?

3 What techniques has the writer used to convert from monologue to dialogue?

4 What is lost or gained in the move from stage script to screenplay?

5 Which of the versions do you prefer? Give your reasons.

6 Write a set of 'Notes for Guidance' which would help another student turn a monologue into a dialogue. Show them to a partner – do they make sense?

5 Choose your own consecutive scenes from the screenplay to turn *back* to a monologue. Following the 'Notes for Guidance' you drafted as part of the previous assignment, write a script for Shirley.

Now perform it for others in your class.

You could extend this into a small drama competition, taking in the rewriting of a short story for the stage or recasting an extract from a play as a short story. As you have seen from the Willy Russell examples, this is not an easy exercise and demands expert writing skills.

6 Read the following film review by Caryn James which first appeared in the *New York Times*. Use a dictionary to sort out any words you are not familiar with.

Shirley Valentine Talks With Others

A heroine whose dialogue can be packed in a tiny publicity pamphlet called 'The Wit and Wisdom of Shirley Valentine' is probably spouting shallow aphorisms rather than anything witty or wise. Banality is precisely the problem with 'Shirley Valentine', the one-woman stage play that has been turned into a misguided, fully cast film.

The single advantage of the drama, on both London and New York stages, was the miraculous performance of Pauline Collins. With warmth and energy, her portrayal of a discontented housewife managed to charm theater audiences and hold their attention for two hours, as her monologue spun dozens of characters and settings out of sheer language. With the illusory power of a magician, Ms Collins even managed to distract the audience from the hackneyed writing in Willy Russell's play.

But the film that opens today at Loews Paramount and other theaters foolishly abandons the singular focus on Ms Collins's sleight of hand or tongue. By adding all the characters and settings that Shirley only talks about on stage, the film reveals the weakness of Mr Russell's script as surely as if a magician's clumsy assistant had pointed a finger at a secret trapdoor. Ms Collins

---

brings as much energy and warmth to the role as ever, but on screen the strength of her performance is shattered by being chopped into tiny, disconnected bits.

Her Shirley is still a 42-year-old Liverpool housewife, slightly plump and believably unglamorous. She spends the first half of the story talking to the kitchen wall – 'Hi'ya, wall,' is an early example of her wit – making chips and eggs for her unappreciative husband and wondering whether she dares to go on a two-week-long vacation to Greece with her best friend, Jane.

•

Now that her two children are grown, Shirley Valentine Bradshaw is suffering from empty-nest syndrome, plain and simple, though Mr Russell treats that phenomenon as if he had made a major scientific discovery. There is little surprise in the fact that Shirley eventually flies to Greece, where she talks to a rock, has a liberating fling with a tavern owner and rediscovers the woman who used to be Shirley Valentine. Or, as she puts it in one of her simplistic slogans, 'I've fallen in love with the idea of living.'

Given the insistent way that Shirley's story is opened up, it is unaccountable that the film's director, Lewis Gilbert, has retained so many awkward traces of the film's theatrical source. Especially in the early sections, Shirley looks directly into the camera and feeds the audience lines that lead to brief flashback scenes. One sequence explains that Jane became a feminist after she found her husband in bed with the milkman. (A large part of Mr Russell's problem is that he does not find this kind of crazy-feminist joke the least bit dated.) But instead of luring us into the film, Ms Collins's glances toward the camera only emphasize the film's disjointedness and artifice.

And as Shirley converses with friends and family, Mr Russell's script turns Ms Collins into a stand-up comedian. Shirley piles one tired punch line on top of another as if her liberation had been tutored by Bob Hope. 'You can't bring logic into this; we're talking about marriage,' she tells Jane, and immediately jumps in with another one-liner as insurance. 'Marriage is like the Middle East; there's no solution.'

•

At least when she arrives in Greece, the scenery is pretty and she is less likely to talk to the camera. There Shirley is too busy paying attention to her Greek lover, played by Tom Conti with an exaggerated accent and an equally exaggerated mustache.

'Shirley Valentine' does include a few redeeming moments. Bernard Hill brings some sympathy to the role of Shirley's oafish husband, who is never mean spirited, only unthinking. And occasionally, as Shirley mourns for the lost possibilities of her 'unused life', Ms Collins brings to the film all the poignant, true emotion that Mr Russell's endless aphorisms try to capture and totally fail to convey. Now and then, she offers a glimpse of the 'Shirley Valentine' that might have been.

Caryn James, *New York Times*

Write a letter to the reviewer in which you express your agreement or disagreement with her views. Having read the extracts above from the stage play will have helped you; if you have seen the film of *Shirley Valentine* you will be in a good position to reply.

Think about the following points as you draft your letter:

- Does film tend to take away from the quality of language used on stage?
- What is lost or gained by a character looking to the camera rather than to a theatre audience?
- Is some of the humour lost on film, in comparison with the theatre?
- Are the Greek scenes likely to work better on film?
- Are the Liverpool 'domestic' scenes likely to be more effective on stage?
- If the camera can say it, the characters don't need to.

▨ In the interview on pages v–xv Willy Russell speaks at length about the differences between writing for the stage and writing for the cinema. Discuss his views, thinking about novels and plays you have read which have been made into films you have seen.

Extra scenes

▨ As the screenplay opens Shirley is talking to her Wall and other parts of her kitchen. Improvise an additional page or two of Shirley's monologue which would fit into the film-script at this point. Think about how frustrated and depressed she is, though always with that comic spirit in her!

▨ Write another film scene featuring Gillian and Shirley. Try to capture some of Gillian's more eccentric habits and Shirley's attitude towards them. Sarcasm or irony would be the comic style to adopt here.

▨ Improvise another couple of scenes which flashback to Young Shirley's schooldays. These could be set in school or at the pub. Then write them up as a scene script.

▣ Imagine Shirley doesn't only meet up with Marjorie Majors but with other school classmates as well. Improvise the scene, twenty years after they have all left school.

▣ Imagine that Shirley has been keeping a diary during the first part of the play, before she leaves for Greece. Draft out a series of diary entries from her point of view, covering the rows with Joe and the preparations for her holiday.

▣ Improvise a conversation between Jane and the other tourists – particularly Dougie and Jeanette – during the course of the plane journey *home* to England. Try to capture Willy Russell's style, perhaps stereotyping their words and reactions to make them seem all the more comic.

▣ As far as the screenplay goes Shirley doesn't seem to have written home to explain her actions. Write two letters from her:
- one to her children, in which she tries to explain her behaviour;
- one to Joe, in which she reflects on their marriage.

▣ Act out a scene between Joe and one of his mates at work in which they discuss what Shirley has done. You could do this in two ways:
- a scene where Joe's mate is sympathetic;
- a scene in which his mate sort of suggests Joe had this coming to him.

▣ With the action of the screenplay over, improvise and then write out – for screen or stage – the following two scenes:
- Brian and Millandra talking about their childhood, their parents' marriage and their predictions for the future;
- Joe and Shirley – a week after they have met up in Mykonos – discussing their future plans.

Shirley Valentine and *Educating Rita*

Educating Rita is another work by Willy Russell that started out on the stage, and was later turned into a film which proved popular with audiences. Essentially, *Educating Rita* is the story of a woman – not unlike Shirley – who left school at fifteen without any formal academic qualifications and who, at the age of twenty-six, decides she wants to study for an Open University degree in English Literature. The progress of her education at the hands of an alcoholic university tutor is the substance of the plot, with Russell constantly encouraging his audience to question what 'education' actually means.

It is easy to see that the two works have some similarities, not least of which is the common backgrounds of Shirley and Rita and their desire to effect some kind of escape from their 'borin' ' husbands and daily chores.

☐ To help you think about Willy Russell as a writer, read the following two extracts from *Educating Rita*. They both come from Act One of the play and reflect Rita's new-found interest in formal education and the barriers she is meeting.

RITA   *I've been realizin' for ages that I was, y' know, slightly out of step. I'm twenty-six. I should have had a baby by now; everyone expects it. I'm sure me husband thinks I'm sterile. He was moanin' all the time, y' know, 'Come off the pill, let's have a baby'. I told him I'd come off it, just to shut him up. But I'm still on it.* (She moves round to Frank*) See, I don't wanna baby yet. See, I wanna discover meself first. Do you understand that?*

FRANK   Yes.

RITA   (moving to the chair up stage of the desk and fiddling with it) *Yeh. They wouldn't round our way. They'd think I was mental. I've tried to explain it to me husband but between you an' me I think he's thick. No, he's not thick, he's blind, he doesn't want to see. You know if I'm readin', or watchin' somethin' different on the telly he gets dead narked, I used to just tell him to piss off but then I realized that it was no good doin' that, that I had to explain to him. I tried to explain that I wanted a better way of livin' me life. An' he listened to me. But he didn't understand because when I'd finished he said he agreed with me and that we should start savin' the money to move off our estate an' get a house out in Formby. Even if it was a new house I wanted I wouldn't go an' live in Formby. I hate that hole, don't you?*

FRANK   *Yes.*

RITA   *Where do you live?*

FRANK   *Formby.*

                        *

FRANK   *What's wrong?* (After a pause) *You know this is getting to be a bit wearisome. When you come to this room you'll do anything except start work immediately. Couldn't you just come in prepared to start work? Where's your essay?*

RITA   (staring out of the window) *I haven't got it.*

FRANK   *You haven't done it?*

RITA   *I said I haven't got it.*

FRANK   *You've lost it?*

RITA   *It's burnt.*

FRANK   *Burnt?*

RITA   *So are all the Chekhov books you lent me. Denny found out I was on the pill again; it was my fault, I left me prescription out. He burnt all me books.*

FRANK   *Oh Christ!*

RITA   *I'm sorry. I'll buy y' some more.*

FRANK   *I wasn't referring to the books. Sod the books.*

RITA   *Why can't he just let me get on with me learnin'? You'd think I was havin' a bloody affair the way he behaves.*

FRANK   *And aren't you?*

       Rita wanders down right. She fiddles with the library steps, smoothing the top step.

RITA   (looking at him) *No. What time have I got for an affair? I'm busy enough findin' meself, let alone findin' someone else. I don't want anyone else. I've begun to find me – an' it's great y' know, it is Frank. It might sound selfish but all I want for the time bein' is what I'm findin' inside me. I certainly don't wanna be rushin' off with some feller, cos the first thing I'll have to do is forget about meself for the sake of him.*

FRANK   *Perhaps, perhaps your husband thinks you're having an affair with me.*

RITA   *Oh go way. You're me teacher. I've told him.*

FRANK   *You've told him about me? What?*

RITA   (sitting down) *I've – tch – I've tried to explain to him how you give me room to breathe. Y' just, like feed me without expectin' anythin' in return.*

FRANK   *What did he say?*

RITA   *He didn't. I was out for a while. When I come back he'd burnt me books an' papers, most of them. I said to him, y' soft get, even if I was havin' an affair there's no point burnin' me books. I'm not havin' it off with Anton Chekhov. He said, 'I wouldn't put it past you to shack up with a foreigner'.*

FRANK   (after a pause) *What are you going to do?*

RITA   *I'll order some new copies for y' an' do the essay again.*

FRANK   *I mean about your husband.*

RITA   (standing up) *I've told him, I said, 'There's no point cryin' over spilt milk, most of the books are gone, but if you touch my* Peer Gynt *I'll kill y'.'*

FRANK   *Tch. Be serious.*

RITA   *I was!*

FRANK   *Do you love him?*

RITA   (after a pause) *I see him lookin' at me sometimes, an' I know what he's thinkin, I do y' know, he's wonderin' where the girl he married has gone to. He even brings me presents sometimes, hopin' that the presents 'll make her come back. But she can't, because she's gone, an' I've taken her place.*

FRANK   *Do you want to abandon this course?*

RITA   *No. No!*

FRANK   *When art and literature begin to take the place of life itself, perhaps it's time to ...*

RITA   (emphatically) *But it's not takin' the place of life, it's providin' me with life itself. He wants to take life away from me; he wants me to stop rockin' the coffin, that's all. Comin' here, doin' this, it's given me more life then I've had in years, an' he should be able to see that. Well, if he doesn't want me when I'm alive I'm certainly not just gonna lie down an' die for him. I told him I'd only have a baby when I had choice. But he doesn't understand. He thinks we've got choice because we can go into a pub that sells eight different kinds of lager. He thinks*

*we've got choice already: choice between Everton an' Liverpool, choosin'
which washin' powder, choosin' between one lousy school an' the next,
between lousy jobs or the dole, choosin' between Stork an' butter.*

Now answer the following questions, first in group discussion and then in
note form:

1 What picture do you get of Rita as a person?

2 What image is created of her husband Denny?

3 What parallels can you draw between the lives of Rita and Shirley?

4 What techniques of comic writing do you see here which remind you of
   Russell's style in *Shirley Valentine*?

5 Which features of the Liverpool dialect appear here, as in *Shirley Valentine*?

6 Are there any lines or phrases which seem to echo between *Educating
   Rita* and *Shirley Valentine*?

☑ Using the thoughts and notes from the above assignment, write an essay
which comments on Willy Russell's style and interests as a writer. The issues
of social class, women's roles, the place of education, escaping reality – all
these should feature in the essay.

Shirley Valentine – the play

The following reviews were first published when the play *Shirley Valentine* –
starring the actress Pauline Collins – first opened at the Vaudeville Theatre,
London, in 1988. It had first been performed at the Everyman Theatre, Liverpool,
in 1986. Remember that these are *not* reviews of the screenplay.

▦ Read through the reviews noting down anything that occurs to you about
their content and style. Use a dictionary to help you understand any vocabulary with which you are not familiar. What, for example, do 'Philistine', 'quasi-
feminist' and 'xenophobic' mean?

WILLY GETS TOP MARKS FOR EDUCATING SHIRLEY

BUYING olive oil in Sainsburys is the nearest Shirley Valentine has got to Greece.

Frying her husband's egg and chips, she ponders on the route that has led to a poky kitchen on a Liverpool housing estate where her only comfort is a glass of wine.

If this sounds like a recipe for another boring, quasi-feminist play, don't despair. The author is Willy Russell who penned *Educating Rita*.

He is a man who knows a thing or two about working-class women trapped in a world from which they yearn to escape.

An offer of a Greek holiday plunges married Shirley Bradshaw into a dilemma.

Should she risk the wrath of her husband Joe, who suffers a culture shock if they go to Chester, and travel on her first holiday abroad?

She knows that the teenage Shirley Valentine would have gone but she has been submerged by marriage, children and humdrum routine.

Joe, she knows, once loved her.

'It's funny though how you treat people you love worse than the people you just like,' she reflects.

So Shirley steels herself and embarks on a holiday with her Cosmopolitan-reading friend Jane. It changes her life.

Pauline Collins turns in a brilliant performance as the Liverpool housewife who finds redemption on a Greek island.

The whole point of the play is Shirley's ordinariness. It's a moving parable for everyone. Bruno Santini's ingenious set focuses on Shirley's prison, the kitchen. Pictures of the other MFI furnished rooms in the house surround it.

It's a clever way of suggesting that the centre of Shirley's world is where Joe's egg and chips are fried.

Director Simon Callow paces this remarkable one-woman show at the Vaudeville Theatre with skill.

Shirley builds a friendship with the audience and we all want her to win.

The St Joan of the fitted units has them cheering in the aisles.

Val Sampson, *Today,*
22 January 1988

An independent spirit

AFTER THE interminable double bill of solo shows by Samuel Beckett and Raymond Cousse at the Donmar Warehouse the other day, I feared that my patience for this form of theatre was exhausted. One-person plays may be excellent value for producers with wages bills to pay, but they only rarely offer audiences a similar degree of satisfaction.

Willy Russell's *Shirley Valentine* at the Vaudeville Theatre is one of the rare exceptions. Pauline Collins holds the stage alone for more than two hours and attention never flags. The play is at times funny, at others desolatingly sad, and at the end it emerges as a moving celebration of the independence of the human spirit.

In an interview, the prolific Russell, whose past successes include *Educating Rita*, the musical *Blood Brothers* and *One for the Road*, still running in the West End, cheekily denied that *Shirley Valentine* was a solo show at all. 'It's quite definitely a play with an otherwise unseen cast,' he maintained, which sounds like mere verbal quibbling until you see the show, and gratefully discover that he is absolutely right.

The scene is the kitchen of Shirley Bradshaw, née Valentine, a 42-year-old Liverpool housewife. As she prepares her husband's supper, and makes inroads into a litre and a half bottle of cheap white wine, she describes her life, often directly addressing the wall, as if it were a father confessor.

Her boorish, xenophobic husband, her feckless children, who have grown up and left home, her neighbour and her best friend, all acquire a vivid life in Miss Collins's sparky monologue, and the jokes are excellent. The play is particularly good on the subject of sex, which Mrs Bradshaw considers to be overrated, like Sainsbury's: 'Just a lot of pushing and shoving, and you still come out with very little in the end.' But the character's pain is palpable, as she considers the loss of youth and the way love has evaporated from her marriage.

All this would be as much as one had any right to expect from a one-woman play, but Russell adds another ingredient, a genuinely absorbing and suspenseful plot. Shirley's friend Jane, who has become a feminist after finding her husband in bed with the milkman, has bought tickets for a holiday in Greece. Will Shirley have the courage to break out of her imprisoning kitchen and rediscover a fulfilled life beyond its walls?

It would be a shame to give away too much of the story, but the humour, human insight and warm sympathy of Russell's script never falter. Miss Collins seizes a gift of a part with both hands, precisely charting her garrulous character's many changes of mood, from despair to open-eyed wonder at the potential richness of life. Simon Callow's assured production does full justice to a fine play.

Charles Spencer, *Daily Telegraph*,
23 January 1988

GREEK ESCAPE

WILLY Russell seems bent on earning himself a reputation as a social agent provocateur encouraging the women of Liverpool to rebel against the lifestyle imposed upon them by their menfolk.

In Educating Rita a working-class girl achieves fresh horizons through adult classes in English literature.

In Shirley Valentine at the Vaudeville the victim of male repression is a 42-year-old housewife who escapes from her domestic cage through discovering the magic of travel.

In some ways Shirley is what Rita might have been had she not been transformed by the excitement of Shakespeare. Trapped by a Philistine husband who is a tyrant about the texture of his fried eggs and the timing of his tea, she despairs of ever getting him to take a holiday abroad because he gets a culture shock if he goes to Chester.

Pauline Collins, alone on the stage throughout the play, talks to herself and to her kitchen wall as she busies herself with her chores.

Her restlessness with her lot stems from her late discovery of the clitoris, her envy of the glamorous life led by a school chum who has become a hooker and her realisation that now that her two children have grown up there is nothing left for her in Liverpool but a gentle descent to the grave.

In a rebellious moment of independence she takes off for Greece with a girlfriend without telling her husband.

Sardonic

Greece lives up to all her fantasies. She acquires a suntan, a happy disposition and a short romantic affair with a local cafe owner. Her ultimate gesture against the empty life of Liverpool is to take a job as a part-time waitress in Greece and presumably make up for all her wasted years by eating moussaka and drinking retsina.

In Pauline Collins, uninhibited about her ample contours in beach clothes, Willy Russell has a Shirley Valentine who interprets his witty and sardonic lines with just the quality of restrained rapture, impatient petulance and light-hearted cynicism that makes the character both credible and delightful.

I am very dubious, however, about Russell's premise that feminine frustration is caused by educational, cultural or national limitations. No doubt in the same seaside town in Greece where Shirley expects to find her Elysium are middle-aged Greek women yearning for the freedom, the welfare comforts and bracing weather of Liverpool.

Milton Shulman, *Standard*, 22 January 1988

Answer the following questions:

1 What does Val Sampson mean when she writes of 'the Liverpool house-wife who finds redemption on a Greek island'?

2 Charles Spencer writes:

> *'It's quite definitely a play with an otherwise unseen cast', he maintained, which sounds like mere verbal quibbling until you see the show, and gratefully discover that he is absolutely right.*

What does the reviewer mean here? Think carefully about your work on the differences between the monologue and screenplay.

3 What is your verdict on Charles Spencer's comment that 'the humour, human insight and warm sympathy of Russell's script never falter'?

4 Milton Shulman writes: 'I am very dubious about Russell's premise that feminine frustration is caused by educational, cultural or national limitations.' What is your view on this statement?

5 What do all three critics say they enjoyed about the play?

6 What criticisms do they make about:
- the production
- the play's content?

7 Which review are you most in sympathy with, and why?

8 Which headline do you think best sums up *Shirley Valentine* as you see it?

9 What do you notice about the style of theatre review writing? Make a short list of the common journalistic techniques.

Shirley Valentine – the film

▣ Look at the following four 'stills' from the Paramount Pictures film *Shirley Valentine*.

Taking each photograph in turn answer the following questions:

- Where in the screenplay does the scene feature?
- What dialogue or 'interior thought' is going on?
- What happens immediately before and after the action shown?
- How do gesture and facial expression contribute to what is happening in the script?
- In what way does the background 'tell its own story'?
- Does the photo match your own image of what the characters and settings should look like?

Suggestions for further reading

Willy Russell

Our Day Out (Hutchinson Educational)
Written for television in 1976, the play chronicles a school outing by a group of Liverpool youngsters. Typical of the author it has both highly amusing and serious moments, posing some interesting questions about discipline and freedom in schools. The stage musical version is available from Methuen Publishers.

Stags and Hens (Methuen Publishers)
Written in 1978, the play is set on the eve before Linda's wedding. The bride-to-be collides with both her old boyfriend (now a rock star) and the 'stag' party of her intended husband — with dramatic consequences. In Linda's character and decision there is a forerunner of both Rita and Shirley Valentine.

The Boy with the Transistor Radio (Hutchinson Educational)
Written for schools' television in 1979, the central character is sixteen-year-old Terry. He is about to leave school but with few employment prospects in inner-city Liverpool. In common with so many of Russell's characters, he dreams of escape — in this case through a dream world created by a radio disc jockey.

Educating Rita (Longman Literature)
Rita's education and 'escape' in the hands of Frank, the alcoholic university tutor, is a clever mix of comedy and pathos. Interesting to compare with *Shirley Valentine*.

Blood Brothers (Methuen Publishers)
A musical which opened at the Liverpool Playhouse in 1983, in which a poor Liverpool mother gives away one of her twin boys at birth to a barren rich women. The boys grow up in different backgrounds but their paths cross at various key times in their lives, with comic and finally tragic results.

Related reading

Pygmalion by Bernard Shaw (Longman Literature)
Its theme of a young flower girl being 'trained up' and 'educated' to pass off as a duchess in high society is fascinating to compare with both *Educating Rita* and *Shirley Valentine*.

Three Plays: A Collier's Friday Night; The Daughter-in-Law; The Widowing of Mrs Holroyd by D H Lawrence (Penguin)
Taken as a collection they offer a powerful insight into a closely knit mining community – with all its family tensions – from which individuals want to escape. Lawrence's use of the Nottinghamshire dialect is interesting to compare with Russell's Liverpool dialect.

Look Back In Anger by John Osborne (Faber)
First seen on the London stage in 1956, it was hailed as 'the best young play of its decade'. A small group of people in their twenties shout out against the older generation's way of doing things and the way they organise society.

The Importance of Being Earnest by Oscar Wilde (Longman Literature)
This famous comedy of errors contains the kind of sharp, verbal repartee which characterises the best of Willy Russell.

Family Circles (Longman Imprint)
This collection contains five radio plays focusing on the joys and problems of family life.

Love and Marriage (Hutchinson)
Six excellent short plays on the collection's theme. Writers include Leonard Kingston and Eric Paice.

Television Comedy Scripts (Longman Imprint)
Includes five 'situation comedies' by a group of popular TV writers, notably Carla Lane and Dick Clement/Ian La Frenais.

P'tang, Yang, Kipperbang (Longman Imprint)
Brings together four television plays by Jack Rosenthal, in which laughter is always *with*, never *at* the characters.

Novels and stories

Sumitra's Story by Rukshana Smith (Bodley Head)
A novel about a young Asian girl growing up in Britain, struggling to throw off her family culture and establish her own identity.

More to Life than Mr Right (Collins)
A collection of short stories which offer challenging views on the search for self-identity amongst contemporary young women.

My Oedipus Complex by Frank O'Connor (Penguin)
A volume of stories which display a knowledge of the feelings and experiences of childhood, together with a marvellous Irish wit.

Bleeding Sinners by Moy McCrory (Methuen)
A collection of tales which have a delightful wit, much of it rooted in Liverpool, and Irish settings very familiar to Willy Russell.

The Ice Is Singing by Jane Rogers (Faber)
A powerful novel about a woman on the run from her husband, her children, and herself.

Wider reading assignments

1 Write a comparative study of the themes and ideas contained within Bernard Shaw's *Pygmalion* and *Educating Rita* and *Shirley Valentine*.

2 From your reading or watching of any plays written largely in dialect, what would you say are the strengths and weaknesses of such plays? What challenges are presented to both the playwright and the audience?

3 Write a review of a couple of plays or films, which you have read or seen, that have given a powerful insight into family life.

4 Jack Rosenthal writes: 'I believe comedy is the best way to learn the truth about ourselves. Maybe it's no accident that human beings are the only animals that laugh.' Write an essay in which you examine how a writer for stage or screen has educated and entertained you simultaneously.

5 Writer Farrukh Dhondy once observed: 'If you have good anti-racist intentions or good 'ist' intentions of any sort, join the appropriate Boy Scout or Girl Guide troupe. Do good works. Don't insult the craft of fiction by reducing it to any form of propaganda.' Has your reading of any of the above titles led you to the conclusion that some writers let their passion for ideas get in the way of telling a good tale?

Write an essay titled 'Fiction or Propaganda', with reference to three books you have read.

Acknowledgements

We are grateful to the following for permission to reproduce copyright material: the author, Sandra Kerr for her poem 'Maintenance Engineer'; Ewan MacNaughton Associates for the article 'An independent spirit' by Charles Spencer from *Daily Telegraph* 23.1.88, © The Daily Telegraph plc; The New York Times Syndication Sales for the article 'Shirley Valentine Talks With Others' by Caryn James from *The New York Times* 30.8.89; News (UK) Ltd for the article 'Willie gets top marks for educating Shirley' by Val Sampson from *Today* 22.1.88; the author's agent for extracts from the play *Educating Rita* by Willy Russell* (Longman Study Text Edition, 1985) & extracts from the play *Shirley Valentine* by Willy Russell*; the author, Daphne Schiller for her poem 'I Had Rather Be a Woman'; Solo Syndication & Literary Agency Ltd for the article 'Greek escape' by Milton Shulman from the *Evening Standard* 22.1.88; The Women's Press Ltd for the poem 'The Washerwoman' from *Fat Like The Sun* by Anna Swir, translated by Grazyna Baran & Margaret Marshment & introduced by the Raving Beauties (pub 1986).

*All rights whatsoever in these plays are strictly reserved and application for performance etc., should be made before rehearsal to Margaret Ramsay Ltd., 14a Goodwin's Court, St. Martin's Lane, London WC2N 4LL. No performance may be given unless a licence has been obtained.

We are grateful to the following for permission to reproduce photographs: Aquarius Picture Library for page 118 and The Ronald Grant Archive for pages 119, 120 and 121.

Cover photograph by The Ronald Grant Archive.

Cover illustration by Andrew Bylo.

Consultant: Geoff Barton.

Longman Group Limited,
Longman House, Burnt Mill, Harlow,
Essex CM20 2JE, England
and Associated Companies throughout the world.

Text of screenplay © W. R. Ltd. 1991
© 1991 Paramount Pictures
This educational edition © Longman Group Limited 1991

First published 1991
Fifth impression 1994

Editorial Material set in 10/12 pt Helvetica Light Condensed

Produced by Longman Singapore Publishers (Pte) Ltd,
Printed in Singapore

ISBN 0 582 08173 4

The Publisher's policy is to use paper manufactured from sustainable forests.

Longman Literature

Series editor: Roy Blatchford

Novels

Jane Austen   *Pride and Prejudice*   0 582 07720 6
Charlotte Brontë   *Jane Eyre*   0 582 07719 2
Emily Brontë   *Wuthering Heights*   0 582 07782 6
Charles Dickens   *Great Expectations*   0 582 07783 4
                      A Christmas Carol   0 582 23664 9
George Eliot   *Silas Marner*   0 582 23662 2
F Scott Fitzgerald   *The Great Gatsby*   0 582 06023 0
                      Tender is the Night   0 582 09716 9
Nadine Gordimer   *July's People*   0 582 06011 7
Graham Greene   *The Captain and the Enemy*   0 582 06024 9
Thomas Hardy   *Far from the Madding Crowd*   0 582 07788 5
                      Tess of the D'Urbervilles   0 582 09715 0
                      The Mayor of Casterbridge   0 582 22586 8
Aldous Huxley   *Brave New World*   0 582 06016 8
Robin Jenkins   *The Cone-Gatherers*   0 582 06017 6
Doris Lessing   *The Fifth Child*   0 582 06021 4
Joan Lindsay   *Picnic at Hanging Rock*   0 582 08174 2
Bernard Mac Laverty   *Lamb*   0 582 06557 7
Brian Moore   *Lies of Silence*   0 582 08170 X
George Orwel   *Animal Farm*   0 582 06010 9
                      Nineteen Eighty-Four   0 582 06018 4
Alan Paton   *Cry, The Beloved Country*   0 582 07787 7
Paul Scott   *Staying On*   0 582 07718 4
Virginia Woolfe   *To the Lighthouse*   0 582 09714 2

Short Stories

Jeffrey Archer   *A Twist in the Tale*   0 582 06022 2
Susan Hill   *A Bit of Singing and Dancing*   0 582 09711 8
Bernard Mac Laverty   *The Bernard Mac Laverty Collection*   0 582 08172 6

Poetry

Five Modern Poets   edited by Barbara Bleiman   0 582 09713 4
Poems From Other Centuries   edited by Adrian Tissier 0 582 22595 X